Rape

Rape
The Power of Consciousness

SUSAN GRIFFIN

PUBLISHED IN SAN FRANCISCO BY
HARPER & ROW, PUBLISHERS
NEW YORK, HAGERSTOWN,
SAN FRANCISCO, LONDON

FIRST EDITION

Designed by Leigh McLellan

Library of Congress Cataloging in Publication Data
Griffin, Susan.
  Rape, the power of consciousness.

  1. Rape—United States. 2. Rape. I. Title.
HV6561.G74   362.8'8   78-20587
ISBN 0-06-250350-2

---

82 83 10 9 8 7 6 5 4 3 2

Contents

Acknowledgments

LET ME FIRST thank Michelle Cliff whose writing and thinking on the work of Simone Weil did much to shape the third essay in this book. Sandy Boucher, who collaborated with me on the last part of the book, was a sensitive reader who pointed out to me much that needed to be said. The final section of the book would never be as it is without the existence of so many women's periodicals, and so let me thank *Quest, Heresies, Chrysalis, Woman Spirit, Ms, Sinister Wisdom, Conditions* and *Signs.* This work would also not have been possible had we not been able to use the Women's History Library as collected by Laura X, part of which is kept on microfilm at the Berkeley Public library. Let me also thank June Jordan and Adrienne Rich for reading and commenting on the third essay in this book and for their support, and Kim Chernin who read this book and helped to make a significant decision with regard to its form. I wish also to thank Gilda Grillo, Lois Sasson, Rezaleah Bat Pinchas and Bob Hoffmann and the Quadrinity Process for their friendship, support and for certain transforming insights which have found their way into this writing. And I am indebted to Julia Dickinson and Bay Area Women Against Rape, to Sandra K. Lambert and the Pennsylvania Coalition Against Rape, and to Melanie Kaye for their help in compiling a list of Rape Crisis Centers for this book. Let me also thank Professor Menachem Amir who consulted with me in 1970 when I wrote the first essay on rape that appears in this book. And finally I would like to thank Marie Cantlon for her intelligent and invaluable editing and for her patience.

In order that we stop being victims, we ourselves must take up the struggle against rape. Individually and collectively we can break the silence and make it no longer a taboo subject, or something shameful which weighs us down.

French witness. *The Proceedings of the International Tribunal on Crimes Against Women.* Diana E. H. Russell and Nicole Van de Ven (Eds.).

Martial arts and self defense study offer a way of self reflection and change . . . I find that I learned the lessons of patriarchy in my muscles and sinews, as well as in my mind and soul; and this martial arts study is both an UNconditioning process, as well as the conditioning and creating of a new self.

Emily Erwin Culpepper, *Womanspirit,* Summer, 1976

She looked up over her knitting and met the third stroke and it seemed to her like her own eyes meeting her own eyes, searching as she could alone search into her mind and her heart, purifying out of existence that lie, any lie. She praised herself in praising the light, without vanity, for she was stern, she was searching, she was beautiful like that light.

Virginia Woolf. *To the Lighthouse*

PART 1

Politics
1971

I

I HAVE NEVER been free of the fear of rape. From a very early age I, like most women, have thought of rape as part of my natural environment—something to be feared and prayed against like fire or lightning. I never asked why men raped; I simply thought it one of the many mysteries of human nature.

I was, however, curious enough about the violent side of humanity to read every crime magazine I was able to ferret away from my grandfather. Each issue featured at least one "sex crime," with pictures of a victim, usually in a pearl necklace, and of the ditch or the orchard where her body was found. I was never certain why the victims were always women, nor what the motives of the murderer were, but I did guess that the world was not a safe place for women. I observed that my grandmother was meticulous about locks, and quick to draw the shades before anyone removed so much as a shoe. I sensed that danger lurked outside.

At the age of eight, my suspicions were confirmed. My grandmother took me to the back of the house where the men wouldn't hear, and told me that strange men wanted to do harm to little girls. I learned not to walk on dark streets, not to talk to strangers, or get into strange cars, to lock doors, and to be modest. She never explained why a man would want to harm a little girl, and I never asked.

If I thought for a while that my grandmother's fears were imaginary, the illusion was brief. That year, on the way home from school, a schoolmate a few years older than I tried to rape me. Later, in an obscure aisle of the local library (while I was reading *Freddy the Pig)* I turned to discover a man exposing himself. Then, the friendly man around the corner was arrested for child molesting.

My initiation to sexuality was typical. Every woman has similar stories to tell—the first man who attacked her may have been a neighbor, a family friend, an uncle, her doctor, or perhaps her own father. And women who grow up in New York City always have tales about the subway.

But though rape and the fear of rape are a daily part of every woman's consciousness, the subject is so rarely discussed by that unofficial staff of male intellectuals (who write the books which study seemingly every other form of male activity) that one begins to suspect a conspiracy of silence. And indeed, the obscurity of rape in print exists in marked contrast to the frequency of rape in reality, for *forcible rape is the most frequently committed violent crime in America today.* The Federal Bureau of Investigation classes three crimes as violent: murder, aggravated assault and forcible rape. In 1968, 31,060 rapes were *reported.* According to the FBI and independent criminologists, however, to approach accuracy this figure must be multiplied by at least a factor of ten to compensate for the fact that most rapes are not reported; when these compensatory mathematics are used, there are more rapes committed than aggravated assaults and homicides.

When I asked Berkeley California's Police Inspector in charge of rape investigation if he knew why men rape women, he replied that he had not spoken with "these people and delved into what really makes them tick, because that really isn't my job. . . ." However, when I asked him how a woman might prevent being raped, he was not so reticent, "I wouldn't advise any female to go walking around alone at night . . . and she should lock her car at all times." The Inspector illustrated his warning with a grisly story about a man who lay in wait for women in the back seats of their cars, while they were shopping in a local supermarket. This man eventually murdered one of his rape victims. "Always lock your car," the Inspector repeated, and then added, without a hint of irony, "Of course, you don't have to be paranoid about this type of thing."

The Inspector wondered why I wanted to write about rape. Like most men he did not understand the urgency of the topic, for, after all, men are not raped. But like most women I had spent considerable time speculating on the true nature of the rapist. When I was very young, my image of the "sexual offender" was a nightmarish amalgamation of the bogey man and Captain Hook: he wore a black cape, and he cackled. As I matured, so did my image of the rapist. Born into the psychoanalytic age, I tried to "understand" the rapist. Rape, I came to believe, was only one of many unfortunate evils produced by sexual repression. Reasoning by tautology, I concluded that any man who would rape a woman must be out of his mind.

Yet, though the theory that rapists are insane is a popular one, this belief has no basis in fact. According to Professor Menachem Amir's study of 646 rape cases in Philadelphia, *Patterns in Forcible Rape,* men who rape are not abnormal. Amir writes, "Studies indicate that sex offenders do not constitute a unique or psychopathological type; nor are they as a group invariably more disturbed than the control groups to which they are compared." Alan Taylor, a parole officer who has worked with rapists in the prison facilities at San Luis Obispo, California, stated the question in plainer language, "Those men were the most normal men there. They had a lot of hang-ups, but they were the same hang-ups as men walking out on the street."

Another canon in the apologetics of rape is that, if it were not for learned social controls, all men would rape. Rape is held to be natural behavior, and not to rape must be learned. But in truth rape is not universal to the human species. Moreover, studies of rape in our culture reveal that, far from being impulsive behavior, most rape is planned. Professor Amir's study reveals that in cases of group rape—(the "gangbang" of masculine slang) 90 percent of the rapes were planned; in pair rapes, 83 percent of the rapes were planned; and in single rapes, 58 percent were planned. These figures should significantly discredit the image of the rapist as a man who is suddenly overcome by sexual needs society does not allow him to fulfill.

Far from the social control of rape being learned, comparisons with other cultures lead one to suspect that, in our society, it is rape itself that is learned. (The fact that rape is against the law should not be considered proof that rape is not in fact encouraged as part of our culture.)

This culture's concept of rape as an illegal, but still understandable, form of behavior is not a universal one. In her study *Sex and Temperament,* Margaret Mead describes a society that does not share our views. The Arapesh do not " . . . have any conception of the male nature that might make rape understandable to them." Indeed our interpretation of rape is a product of our conception of the nature of male sexuality. A common retort to the question, why don't women rape men, is the myth that men have greater sexual needs, that their sexuality is more urgent than women's. And it is the nature of human beings to want to live up to what is expected of them.

And this same culture which expects aggression from the male expects passivity from the female. Conveniently, the companion myth about the nature of female sexuality is that all women secretly want to be raped. Lurking beneath her modest female exterior is a subconscious desire to be ravished. The following description of a stag movie, written by Brenda Starr in Los Angeles' underground paper, *Everywoman,* typifies this male fantasy. The movie "showed a woman in her underclothes reading on her bed. She is interrupted by a rapist with a knife. He immediately wins her over with his charm and they get busy sucking and fucking." An advertisement in the *Berkeley Barb* reads, "Now as all women know from their daydreams, rape has a lot of advantages. Best of all it's so simple. No preparation necessary, no planning ahead of time, no wondering if you should or shouldn't; just whang! bang!" Thanks to Masters and Johnson even the scientific canon recognizes that for the female, "whang! bang!" can scarcely be described as pleasurable.

Still, the male psyche persists in believing that, protestations and struggles to the contrary, deep inside her mysterious feminine soul, the female victim has wished for her own fate. A young woman who was raped by the husband of a friend said that days after the incident the man returned to her home, pounded on the door and screamed to her, "Jane, Jane. You loved it. You know you loved it."

The theory that women like being raped extends itself by deduction into the proposition that most or much of rape is provoked by the victim. But this too is only myth. Though provocation, considered a mitigating factor in a court of law, may consist of only "a gesture," according to the Federal Commission on Crimes of Violence, only 4 percent of reported rapes involved any precipitative behavior by the woman.

The notion that rape is enjoyed by the victim is also convenient for the man who, though he would not commit forcible rape, enjoys the idea of its existence, as if rape confirms that enormous sexual potency which he secretly knows to be his own. It is for the pleasure of the armchair rapist that detailed accounts of violent rapes exist in the media. Indeed, many men appear to take sexual pleasure from nearly all forms of violence. Whatever the motivation, male sexuality and violence in our culture seem to be inseparable. James Bond alternately whips out his revolver and his cock, and though there is no known connection between the skills of gunfighting and lovemaking, pacifism seems suspiciously effeminate.

In a recent fictional treatment of the Manson case, Frank Conroy writes of his vicarious titillation when describing the murders to his wife:

"Every single person there was killed." She didn't move.
"It sounds like there was torture," I said. As the words left my mouth I knew there was no need to say them to frighten her into believing that she needed me for protection.

The pleasure he feels as his wife's protector is inextricably mixed with pleasure in the violence itself. Conroy writes, "I was excited by the killings, as one excited by castastrophe on a grand scale, as one is alert to pre-echoes of unknown changes, hints of unrevealed secrets, rumblings of chaos. . . ."

The attraction of the male in our culture to violence and death is a tradition Manson and his admirers are carrying on with tireless avidity (even presuming Manson's innocence, he dreams of the purification of fire and destruction). It was Malraux in his *Anti-Memoirs* who said that, for the male, facing death was the illuminating experience analogous to childbirth for the female. Certainly our culture does glorify war and shroud the agonies of the gunfighter in veils of mystery.

And in the spectrum of male behavior, rape, the perfect combination of sex and violence, is the penultimate act. Erotic pleasure cannot be separated from culture, and in our culture male eroticism is wedded to power. Not only should a man be taller and stronger than a female in the perfect love-match, but he must also demonstrate his superior strength in gestures of dominance which are perceived as amorous. Though the law attempts to make a clear division between rape and sexual intercourse, in fact the courts find it difficult to distinguish between a case where the decision to copulate was mutual and one where a man forced himself upon his partner.

The scenario is even further complicated by the expectation that, not only does a woman mean "yes" when she says "no," but that a really decent woman ought to begin by saying "no," and then be led down the primrose path to acquiescence. Ovid, the author of Western Civilization's most celebrated sex manual, makes this expectation perfectly clear:

> ... and when I beg you to say "yes," say "no." Then let me lie outside your bolted door. ... So Love grows strong. ...

That the basic elements of rape are involved in all heterosexual relationships may explain why men often identify with the offender in this crime. But to regard the rapist as the victim, a man driven by his inherent sexual needs to take what will not be given him, reveals a basic ignorance of sexual politics. For in our culture heterosexual love finds an erotic expression through male dominance and female submission. A man who derives pleasure from raping a woman clearly must enjoy force and dominance as much or more than the simple pleasures of the flesh. Coitus cannot be experienced in isolation. The weather, the state of the nation, the level of sugar in the blood—all will affect a man's ability to achieve orgasm. If a man can achieve sexual pleasure after terrorizing and humiliating the object of his passion, and in fact while inflicting pain upon her, one must assume he derives pleasure directly from terrorizing, humiliating and harming a woman. According to Amir's study of forcible rape, on a statistical average the man who has been convicted of rape was found to have a normal sexual personality, tending to be different from the normal, well-adjusted male only in having a greater tendency to express violence and rage.

And if the professional rapist is to be separated from the average dominant heterosexual, it may be mainly a quantitative difference. For the existence of rape as an index to masculinity is not entirely metaphorical. Though this measure of masculinity seems to be more publicly exhibited among "bad boys" or aging bikers who practice sexual initiation through group rape, in fact, "good boys" engage in the same rites to prove their manhood. In Stockton, a small town in California which epitomizes silent-majority America, a bachelor party was given last summer for a young man about to be married. A woman was hired to dance "topless" for the amusement of the guests. At the high point of the evening the bridegroom-to-be dragged the woman into a bedroom. No move was made by any of his companions to stop what was clearly going to be an attempted rape. Far from it. As the woman described, "I tried to keep him away—told him of my Herpes Genitalis, et cetera, but he couldn't face the guys if he didn't screw me." After the bridegroom had finished raping the woman and returned with her to the party, far from chastising him, his friends heckled the woman and covered her with wine.

It was fortunate for the dancer that the bridegroom's friends did not follow him into the bedroom for, though one might suppose that in group rape, since the victim is outnumbered, less force would be inflicted on her, in fact, Amir's studies indicate, "the most excessive degrees of violence occurred in group rape." Far from discouraging violence, the presence of other men may in fact encourage sadism, and even cause the behavior. In an unpublished study of group rape by Gilbert Geis and Duncan Chappell, the authors refer to a study by W. H. Blanchard which relates,

> The leader of the male group . . . apparently precipitated and maintained the activity, despite misgivings, because of a need to fulfill the role that the other two men had assigned to him. "I was scared when it began to happen," he says. "I wanted to leave but I didn't want to say it to the other guys—you know—that I was scared."

Thus it becomes clear that not only does our culture teach men the rudiments of rape, but society, or more specifically other men, encourage the practice of it.

II

> *Every man I meet wants to protect me. Can't figure out what from.*
> —Mae West

If a male society rewards aggressive, domineering sexual behavior, it contains within itself a sexual schizophrenia. For the masculine man is also expected to prove his mettle as a protector of women. To the naive eye, this dichotomy implies that men fall into one of two categories: those who rape and those who protect. In fact, life does not prove so simple. In a study euphemistically entitled "Sex Aggression by College Men," it was discovered that men who believe in a double standard of morality for men and women, who in fact believe most fervently in the ultimate value of virginity, are more liable to commit "this aggressive variety of sexual exploitation."

(At this point in our narrative it should come as no surprise that Sir Thomas Malory, creator of that classic tale of chivalry, *The Knights of the Round Table,* was himself arrested and found guilty for repeated incidents of rape.)

In the system of chivalry, men protect women against men. This is not unlike the protection relationship which the mafia established with small businesses in the early part of this century. Indeed, chivalry is an age-old protection racket which depends for its existence on rape.

According to the male mythology which defines and perpetuates rape, it is an animal instinct inherent in the male. The story goes that sometime in our pre-historical past, the male, more hirsute and burly than today's counterparts, roamed about an uncivilized landscape until he found a desirable female. (Oddly enough, this female is *not* pictured as more muscular than the modern woman.) Her mate does not bother with courtship. He simply grabs her by the hair and drags her to the closest cave. Presumably, one of the major advantages of modern civilization for the female has been the civilizing of the male. We call it chivalry.

But women do not get chivalry for free. According to the logic of sexual politics, we too have to civilize our behavior. (Enter chastity. Enter virginity. Enter monogamy.) For the female, civilized behavior means chastity before marriage and faithfulness within it. Chivalrous behavior in the male is supposed to protect that chastity from involuntary defilement. The fly in the ointment of this otherwise peaceful system is the fallen woman. She does not behave. And therefore she does not deserve protection. Or, to use another argument, a major tenet of the same value system: what has once been defiled cannot again be violated. One begins to suspect that it is the behavior of the fallen woman, and not that of the male, that civilization aims to control.

The assumption that a woman who does not respect the double standard deserves whatever she gets (or at the very least "asks for it") operates in the courts today. While in some states a man's previous rape convictions are not considered admissible evidence, the sexual reputation of the rape victim is considered a crucial element of the facts upon which the court must decide innocence or guilt.

The court's respect for the double standard manifested itself particularly clearly in the case of the People v. Jerry Plotkin. Mr. Plotkin, a 36-year-old jeweler, was tried for rape last spring in a San Francisco Superior Court. According to the woman who brought the charges, Plotkin, along with three other men, forced her at gunpoint to enter a car one night in October 1970. She was taken to Mr. Plotkin's fashionable apartment where he and the three other men first raped her and then, in the delicate language of the *S.F. Chronicle,* "subjected her to perverted sex acts." She was, she said, set free in the morning with the warning that she would be killed if she spoke to anyone about the event. She did report the incident to the police who then searched Plotkin's apartment and discovered a long list of names of women. Her name was on the list and had been crossed out.

In addition to the woman's account of her abduction and rape, the prosecution submitted four of Plotkin's address books containing the names of hundreds of women. Plotkin claimed he did not know all of the women since some of the names had been given to him by friends and he had not yet called on them. Several women, however, did testify in court that Plotkin had, to cite the *Chronicle,* "lured them up to his apartment under one pretext or another, and forced his sexual attentions on them."

Plotkin's defense rested on two premises. First, through his own testimony Plotkin established a reputation for himself as a sexual libertine who frequently picked up girls in bars and took them to his house where sexual relations often took place. He was the Playboy. He claimed that the accusation of rape, therefore, was false—this incident had simply been one of many casual sexual relationships, the victim one of many playmates. The second premise of the defense was that his accuser was also a sexual libertine. However, the picture created of the young woman (fully 13 years younger than Plotkin) was not akin to the light-hearted, gay-bachelor image projected by the defendant. On the contrary, the day after the defense cross-examined the woman, the *Chronicle* printed a story headlined,

"Grueling Day For Rape Case Victim." (A leaflet passed out by women in front of the courtroom was more succinct, "rape was committed by four men in a private apartment in October; on Thursday, it was done by a judge and a lawyer in a public courtroom.")

Through skillful questioning fraught with innuendo, Plotkin's defense attorney James Martin MacInnis portrayed the young woman as a licentious opportunist and unfit mother. MacInnis began by asking the young woman (then employed as a secretary) whether or not it was true that she was "familiar with liquor" and had worked as a "cocktail waitress." The young woman replied (the *Chronicle* wrote "admitted") that she had worked once or twice as a cocktail waitress. The attorney then asked if she had worked as a secretary in the financial district but had "left that employment after it was discovered that you had sexual intercourse on a couch in the office." The woman replied, "That is a lie. I left because I didn't like working in a one-girl office. It was too lonely." Then the defense asked if, while working as an attendant at a health club, "you were accused of having a sexual affair with a man?" Again the woman denied the story, "I was never accused of that."

Plotkin's attorney then sought to establish that his client's accuser was living with a married man. She responded that the man was separated from his wife. Finally he told the court that she had "spent the night" with another man who lived in the same building.

At this point in the testimony the woman asked Plotkin's defense attorney, "Am I on trial? . . . It is embarrassing and personal to admit these things to all these people. . . . I did not commit a crime. I am a human being." The lawyer, true to the chivalry of his class, apologized and immediately resumed questioning her, turning his attention to her children. (She is divorced, and the children at the time of the trial were in a foster home.) "Isn't it true that your two children have a sex game in which one gets on top of another and they—"That is a lie!" the young woman interrupted him. She ended her testimony by explaining "They are wonderful children. They are not perverted."

The jury, divided in favor of acquittal ten to two, asked the court stenographer to read the woman's testimony back to them. After this reading, the Superior Court acquitted the defendant of both charges of rape and kidnapping.

According to the double standard a woman who has had sexual intercourse out of wedlock cannot be raped. Rape is not only a crime of aggression against the body; it is a transgression against chastity as defined by men. When a woman is forced into a sexual relationship, she has, according to the male ethos, been violated. But she is also defiled if she does not behave according to the double standard, by maintaining her chastity, or confining her sexual activities to a monogamous relationship.

One should not assume, however, that a woman can avoid the possibility of rape simply by behaving. Though myth would have it that mainly "bad girls" are raped, this theory has no basis in fact. Available statistics would lead one to believe that a safer course is promiscuity. In a study of rape done in the District of Columbia, it was found that 82 percent of the rape victims had a "good reputation." Even the Police Inspector's advice to stay off the streets is rather useless, for almost half of reported rapes occur in the home of the victim and are committed by a man she has never before seen. Like indiscriminate terrorism, rape can happen to any woman, and few women are ever without this knowledge.

But the courts and the police, both dominated by white males, continue to suspect the rape victim, *sui generis,* of provoking or asking for her own assault. According to Amir's study, the police tend to believe that a woman without a good reputation cannot be raped. The rape victim is usually submitted to countless questions about her own sexual mores and behavior by the police. This preoccupation is partially justified by the legal requirements for prosecution in a rape case. The rape victim must have been penetrated, and she must have made it clear to her assailant that she did not want penetration (unless of course she is unconscious). A refusal to accompany a man to some isolated place to allow him to touch her does not in the eyes of the court, constitute rape. She must have said "no" at the crucial genital moment. And the rape victim, to qualify as such, must also have put up a physical struggle—unless she can prove that to do so would have been to endanger her life.

But the zealous interest the police frequently exhibit in the physical details of a rape case is only partially explained by the requirements of the court. A woman who was raped in Berkeley was asked to tell the story of her rape four different times "right out in the street," while her assailant was escaping. She was then required to submit to a pelvic examination to prove that penetration had taken place. Later, she was taken to the police station where she was asked the same questions again: "Were you forced?" "Did he penetrate?" "Are you sure your life was in danger and you had no other choice?" This woman had been pulled off the street by a man who held a 10-inch knife at her throat and forcibly raped her. She was raped at midnight and was not able to return to her home until five in the morning. Police contacted her twice again in the next week, once by telephone at two in the morning and once at four in the morning. In her words, "The rape was probably the least traumatic incident of the whole evening. If I'm ever raped again, . . . I wouldn't report it to the police because of all the degradation. . . ."

If white women are subjected to unnecessary and often hostile questioning after having been raped, third world women are often not believed at all. According to the white male ethos (which is not only sexist but racist), third world women are defined from birth as "impure." Thus the white male is provided with a pool of women who are fair game for sexual imperialism. Third world women frequently do not report rape and for good reason. When blues singer Billie Holliday was 10 years old, she was taken off to a local house by a neighbor and raped. Her mother brought the police to rescue her, and she was taken to the local police station crying and bleeding:

> When we got there, instead of treating me and Mom like somebody who called the cops for help, they treated me like I'd killed somebody. . . . I guess they had me figured for having enticed this old goat into the whorehouse. . . . All I know for sure is they threw me into a cell . . . a fat white matron . . . saw I was still bleeding, she felt sorry for me and gave me a couple glasses of milk. But nobody else did anything for me except give me filthy looks and snicker to themselves.
>
> After a couple of days in a cell they dragged me into a court. Mr. Dick got sentenced to five years. They sentenced me to a Catholic institution.

Clearly the white man's chivalry is aimed only to protect the chastity of "his" women.

As a final irony, that same system of sexual values from which chivalry is derived has also provided womankind with an unwritten code of behavior, called femininity, which makes a feminine woman the perfect victim of sexual aggression. If being chaste does not ward off the possibility of assault, being feminine certainly increases the chances that it will succeed. To be submissive is to defer to masculine strength; is to lack muscular development or any interest in defending oneself; is to let doors be opened, to have one's arm held when crossing the street. To be feminine is to wear shoes which make it difficult to run; skirts which inhibit one's stride; underclothes which inhibit the circulation. Is it not an intriguing observation that those very clothes which are thought to be flattering to the female and attractive to the male are those which make it impossible for a woman to defend herself against aggression?

Each girl as she grows into womanhood is taught fear. Fear is the form in which the female internalizes both chivalry and the double standard. Since, biologically speaking, women in fact have the same if not greater potential for sexual expression as do men, the woman who is taught that she must behave differently from a man must also learn to distrust her own carnality. She must deny her own feelings and learn not to act from them. She fears herself. This is the essence of passivity and, of course, a woman's passivity is not simply sexual but functions to cripple her from self-expression in every area of her life.

Passivity itself prevents a woman from ever considering her own potential for self-defense and forces her to look to men for protection. The woman is taught fear, but this time fear of the other; and yet her only relief from this fear is to seek out the other. Moreover, the passive woman is taught to regard herself as impotent, unable to act, unable even to perceive, in no way self-sufficient, and finally, as the object and not the subject of human behavior. It is in this sense that a woman is deprived of the status of a human being. She is not free to be.

III

Since Ibsen's Nora slammed the door on her patriarchical husband, woman's attempt to be free has been more or less fashionable. In this nineteenth-century portrait of a woman leaving her marriage, Nora tells her husband, "Our home has been nothing but a playroom. I have been your doll-wife just as at home I was papa's doll-child." And, at least on the stage, "The Doll's House" crumbled, leaving audiences with hope for the fate of the modern woman. And today, as in the past, womankind has not lacked examples of liberated women to emulate: Emma Goldman, Greta Garbo and Isadora Duncan all denounced marriage and the double standard, and believed their right to freedom included sexual independence; but still their example has not affected the lives of millions of women who continue to marry, divorce and remarry, living out their lives dependent on the status and economic power of men. Patriarchy still holds the average woman prisoner not because she lacks the courage of an Isadora Duncan, but because the material conditions of her life prevent her from being anything but an object.

In the *Elementary Structures of Kinship,* Claude Levi-Strauss gives to marriage this universal description, "It is always a system of exchange that we find at the origin of the rules of marriage." In this system of exchange, a woman is the "most precious possession." Levi-Strauss continues that the custom of including women as booty in the marketplace is still so general that "a whole volume would not be sufficient to enumerate instances of it." Levi-Strauss makes it clear that he does not exclude Western Civilization from his definition of "universal" and cites examples from modern wedding ceremonies. (The marriage ceremony is still one in which the husband and wife become one, and "that one is the husband.")

The legal proscription against rape reflects this possessory view of women. An article in the 1952–53 *Yale Law Journal* describes the legal rationale behind laws against rape:

> In our society sexual taboos, often enacted into law, buttress a system of monogamy based upon the law of "free bargaining" of the potential spouses. Within this process the woman's power to withhold or grant sexual access is an important bargaining weapon.

Presumably then, laws against rape are intended to protect the right of a woman, not for physical self-determination, but for physical "bargaining." The article goes on to explain explicitly why the preservation of the bodies of women is important to men:

> The consent standard in our society does more than protect a significant item of social currency for women; it fosters, and is in turn bolstered by, a masculine pride in the exclusive possession of a sexual object. The consent of a woman to sexual intercourse awards the man a privilege of bodily access, a personal "prize," whose value is enhanced by sole owner-

ship. An additional reason for the man's condemnation of rape may be found in the threat to his status from a decrease in the "value" of his sexual possession which would result from forcible violation.

The passage concludes by making clear whose interest the law is designed to protect. "The man responds to this undercutting of his status as *possessor* of the girl with hostility toward the rapist; no other restitution device is available. The law of rape provides an orderly outlet for his vengeance." Presumably the female victim in any case will have been sufficiently socialized so as not to consciously feel any strong need for vengeance. If she does feel this need, society does not speak to it.

The laws against rape exist to protect rights of the male as possessor of the female body, and not the right of the female over her own body. Even without this enlightening passage from the *Yale Law Review,* the laws themselves are clear: In no state can a man be accused of raping his wife. How can any man steal what already belongs to him? It is in the sense of rape as theft of another man's property that Kate Millett writes, "Traditionally rape has been viewed as an offense one male commits against another—a matter of abusing his woman." In raping another man's woman, a man may aggrandize his own manhood and concurrently reduce that of another man. Thus a man's honor is not subject directly to rape, but only indirectly, through "his" woman.

If the basic social unit is the family, in which the woman is a possession of her husband, the superstructure of society is a male hierarchy, in which men dominate other men (or patriarchal families dominate other patriarchal families). And it is no small irony that, while the very social fabric of our male-dominated culture denies women equal access to political, economic and legal power, the literature, myth and humor of our culture depict women not only as the power behind the throne, but the real source of the oppression of men. The religious version of this fairy tale blames Eve for both carnality and eating of the tree of knowledge, at the same time making her gullible to the obvious devices of a serpent. Adam, of course, is merely the trusting victim of love. Certainly this is a biased story. But no more biased than the one television audiences receive today from the latest slick comedians. Through a media which is owned by men, censored by a state dominated by men, all the evils of this social system which make a man's life unpleasant are blamed upon "the wife." The theory is: were it not for the female who waits and plots to "trap" the male into marriage, modern man would be able to achieve Olympian freedom. She is made the scapegoat for a system which is in fact run by men.

Nowhere is this more clear than in the white racist use of the concept of white womanhood. The white male's open rape of black women, coupled with his overweening concern for the chastity and protection of his wife and daughters, represents an extreme of sexist and racist hypocrisy. While on the one hand she was held up as the standard for purity and virtue, on the other the Southern white woman was never asked if she wanted to be on a pedestal, and in fact any deviance from the male-defined standards for white womanhood was treated severely. (It is a powerful commentary on American racism that the historical role of Blacks as slaves, and thus possessions without power, has robbed black women of legal and economic protection through marriage. Thus black women in Southern society and in the ghettoes of the North have long been easy game for white rapists.) The fear that black men would rape white women was classic paranoia. Quoting from Ann Breen's unpublished study of racism and sexism in the South, *"The New South: White Man's Country,"* Frederick Douglass legitimately points out that, had the black man wished to rape white women, he had ample opportunity to do so during the Civil War when white women, the wives, sisters, daughters and mothers of the rebels, were left in the care of Blacks. But yet not a single act of rape was committed during this time. The Ku Klux Klan, who tarred and feathered black men and lynched them in the honor of the purity of white womanhood, also applied tar and feathers to a Southern white woman accused of bigamy, which leads one to suspect that Southern white men were not so much outraged at the violation of the woman as a person, in the few instances where rape was actually committed by black men, but at the violation of his property rights. In the situation where a black man was found to be having sexual relations with a white woman, the white woman could exercise skin-privilege, and claim that she had been raped in which case the black man was lynched. But if she did not claim rape, she herself was subject to lynching.

In constructing the myth of white womanhood so as to justify the lynching and oppression of black men and women, the white male

has created a convenient symbol of his own power which has result-
ed in black hostility toward the white "bitch," accompanied by a
fear on the part of many white women of the black rapist. Moreover,
it is not surprising that after being told for two centuries that he
wants to rape white women, black men have begun to actually commit that act. But it is crucial to note that the frequency of this practice is outrageously exaggerated in the white mythos. Ninety percent of reported rape is intra- not inter-racial.

In *Soul on Ice,* Eldridge Cleaver has described the mixing of a
rage against white power with the internalized sexism of a black
man raping a white woman.

> Somehow I arrived at the conclusion that, as a matter of principle, it
> was of paramount importance for me to have an antagonistic, ruthless at-
> titude toward white women. . . . Rape was an insurrectionary act. It de-
> lighted me that I was defying and trampling upon the white man's law,
> upon his system of values and that I was defiling his women—and this
> point, I believe, was the most satisfying to me because I was very resent-
> ful over the historical fact of how the white man has used the black wom-
> an.

Thus a black man uses white women to take out his rage against
white men. But, in fact, whenever a rape of a white woman by a
black man does take place, it is again the white man who benefits.
First, the act itself terrorizes the white woman and makes her more
dependent on the white male for protection. Then, if the woman
prosecutes her attacker, the white man is afforded legal opportunity
to exercise overt racism. Of course, the knowledge of the rape helps
to perpetuate two myths which are beneficial to white male rule—
the bestiality of the black man and the desirability of white women.
Finally, the white man surely benefits because he himself is not the
object of attack—he has been allowed to stay in power.

Indeed, the existence of rape in any form is beneficial to the rul-
ing class of white males. For rape is a kind of terrorism which severely limits the freedom of women and makes women dependent on
men. Moreover, in the act of rape, the rage that one man may harbor toward another higher in the male hierarchy can be deflected
toward a female scapegoat. For every man there is always someone
lower on the social scale on whom he can take out his aggressions.
And that is any woman alive.

This oppressive attitude towards women finds its institutionalization in the traditional family. For it is assumed that a man "wears the pants" in his family—he exercises the option of rule whenever he so chooses. Not that he makes all the decisions—clearly women make most of the important day-to-day decisions in a family. But when a conflict of interest arises, it is the man's interest which will prevail. His word, in itself, is more powerful. He lords it over his wife in the same way his boss lords it over him, so that the very process of exercising his power becomes as important an act as obtaining whatever it is his power can get for him. This notion of power is key to the male ego in this culture, for the two acceptable measures of masculinity are a man's power over women and his power over other men. A man may boast to his friends that "I have 20 men working for me." It is also aggrandizement of his ego if he has the financial power to clothe his wife in furs and jewels. And, if a man lacks the wherewithal to acquire such power, he can always express his rage through equally masculine activities—rape and theft. Since male society defines the female as a possession, it is not surprising that the felony most often committed together with rape is theft. As the following classic tale of rape points out, the elements of theft, violence and forced sexual relations merge into an indistinguishable whole.

The woman who told the following story was acquainted with the man who tried to rape her. When the man learned that she was going to be staying alone for the weekend, he began early in the day a polite campaign to get her to go out with him. When she continued to refuse his request, his chivalrous mask dropped away:

> I had locked all the doors because I was afraid, and I don't know how he got in; it was probably through the screen door. When I woke up, he was shaking my leg. His eyes were red, and I knew he had been drinking or smoking. I thought I would try to talk my way out of it. He started by saying that he wanted to sleep with me, and then he got angrier and angrier, until he started to say, "I want pussy," "I want pussy." Then, I got scared and tried to push him away. That's when he started to force himself on me. It was awful. It was the most humiliating, terrible feeling. He was forcing my legs apart and ripping my clothes off. And it was painful. I did fight him—he was slightly drunk and I was able to keep him away. I had taken judo a few years back, but I was afraid to throw a chop for fear that he'd kill me. I could see he was getting more and more violent. I was thinking wildly of some way to get out of this alive, and then I said to him, "Do you want money? I'll give you money." We had money but I

was also thinking that if I got to the back room I could telephone the police—as if the police would have even helped. It was a stupid thing to think of because obviously he would follow me. And he did. When he saw me pick up the phone, he tried to tie the cord around my neck. I screamed at him that I did have the money in another room, that I was going to call the police because I was scared, but that I would never tell anybody what happened. It would be an absolute secret. He said, "okay," and I went to get the money. But when he got it, all of a sudden he got this crazy look in his eye and he said to me, "Now I'm going to kill you." Then I started saying my prayers. I knew there was nothing I could do. He started to hit me—I still wasn't sure if he wanted to rape me at this point—or just to kill me. He was hurting me, but hadn't yet gotten me into a stranglehold because he was still drunk and off balance. Somehow we pushed into the kitchen where I kept looking at this big knife. But I didn't pick it up. Somehow, no matter how much I hated him at that moment, I still couldn't imagine putting the knife in his flesh, and then I was afraid he would grab it and stick it into me. Then he was hitting me again and somehow we pushed through the back door of the kitchen and onto the porch steps. We fell down the steps and that's when he started to strangle me. He was on top of me. He just went on and on until finally I lost consciousness. I did scream, though my screams sounded like whispers to me. But what happened was that a cab driver happened by and frightened him away. The cab driver revived me—I was out only a minute at the most. And then I ran across the street and I grabbed the woman who was our neighbor and screamed at her, "Am I alive? Am I still alive?"

Rape is an act of aggression in which the victim is denied her self-determination. It is an act of violence which, if not actually followed by beatings or murder, nevertheless always carries with it the threat of death. And finally, rape is a form of mass terrorism, for the victims of rape are chosen indiscriminately, but the propagandists for male supremacy broadcast that it is women who cause rape by being unchaste or in the wrong place at the wrong time—in essence, by behaving as though they were free.

The threat of rape is used to deny women employment. (In California, the Berkeley Public Library, until pushed by the Federal Employment Practices Commission, refused to hire female shelvers because of perverted men in the stacks.) The fear of rape keeps women off the streets at night. Keeps women at home. Keeps women passive and modest for fear that they be thought provocative.

It is part of human dignity to be able to defend oneself, and women are learning. Some women have learned karate; some to shoot guns. And yet we will not be free until the threat of rape and the atmosphere of violence is ended, and to end that the nature of male behavior must change.

But rape is not an isolated act that can be rooted out from patriarchy without ending patriarchy itself. The same men and power structure who victimize women are engaged in the act of raping Vietnam, raping Black people and the very earth we live upon. Rape is a classic act of domination where, in the words of Kate Millett, "the emotions of hatred, contempt, and the desire to break or violate personality," take place. This breaking of the personality characterizes modern life itself. No simple reforms can eliminate rape. As the symbolic expression of the white male hierarchy, rape is the quintessential act of our civilization, one which, Valerie Solanis warns, is in danger of "humping itself to death."

PART 2

A History
1971-1978

I

1971. FOR ME a year of rages. We rose like a chorus of Erinyes. The furies. All that had been held back, the stories we never told; what we did not see or refused to recognize. And none of us alone in this. Now any woman, a neighbor, one's blood relatives, strangers had become allies, part of an unspoken network of thought. A whole new connective tissue began to grow between each of us and the women around us and a past we now claimed as our own and the lives of our daughters, or girls unborn which we wanted to imagine as different from our own, unscarred, not damaged by the list of atrocities we could suddenly now name.

And what is to be remembered is that before this eight years we have lived through since, much of what was the actuality of our lives went unnamed. We did not speak of rape. If a woman was raped she was supposed to feel ashamed. She *was* shamed. The very atmosphere around her said that she had been violated and damaged like property, that she must have wanted this rape, drawn this to her. And the atmosphere, like rape itself, seemed as if it had existed forever, were a natural phenomenon, and not made up of man-made assumptions and prejudices born of a particular social reality.

And so sending her words into this field, Germaine Greer argued

that women do not want rape, had to justify her fear of a child mo-
lester as a girl with a quotation from Eldridge Cleaver, describing
rape as "bloody, hateful, bitter and malignant." And my own words
were bent and strained in the same way. I become tired even thinking of the labors with which I struggled with propriety and assumption in my own mind. Feeling the need to prove that rape was not an
event we were bound to accept through the natural order, I pointed
to cultures in which rape was a totally foreign concept; as if the fear
of rape were simply a woman's paranoia, I quoted statistics which
proved how often women are raped. Over and over in different ways
I had to work against a mountain of argumentation that in one way
or another apologized for rape, arguments that women desire rape,
that rapists are victims of sexual repression, overwhelmed by bodily
needs, that accusations of rape are merely projections of female fantasy. At its heart, the whole issue of rape seemed to revolve around
whether or not one could trust a woman's word; and behind this
questioning of our word, whether one could trust a woman's being,
whether we could *trust our own being*.

And yes, studies are still being done seeking to prove that women
want to be raped or cause their own rapes. Pornography, and a kind
of subtle, ingrained pornographic culture surround us with images
of women who seek domination, humiliation, enslavement, who take
pleasure in these states. But I am no longer impassioned to argue
with anyone that women do not seek pain, that we do not want to be
raped; that we do not cause our own rapes. Because in this last eight
years (between the writing of the first and second essays in this
book), we have created another culture for ourselves—a refuge in
which women's words are believed—and we can experience the
truth of ourselves in words and images. This is a place of the mind,
but still a place, made by bent and strained words, so that now, our
words do not have to be so bent, so strained.

Now, writing from this place, I want more than the mere unmask-
ing or naming of atrocity. I have lived in a free place, and my head
is filled with different visions. I am trying to think of a world in
which rape would be a foreign concept. What would that world be?
How would I be different if rape never existed?

But how did we come to envision a world without rape? For to assume that such a world can exist is an amazing departure from a
past we all share which told us rape was as inevitable and inalterable

as rainstorms in our lives. To dream of a world without rape is to dream of indeed a radically different world.

That world of 1970 did not give birth to such dreams: so much in the way of assumption would have to be wiped away, a whole field cleared for such visions to grow. For the issue of rape was in no way ever separate from the question of the whole liberation of women as we had been defined by patriarchy, and we did not see it as separate. To begin with, for us to begin to protest against rape we had to see that there was such a thing as a patriarchy, and once seeing patriarchy, other conditions became visible to us, and other lies about these conditions. We knew that we were not the protected and thoughtless beings whom men saw in our places. We knew our own sexuality, our own feelings about motherhood, work, our spirits. We knew we would not perish without men or marriage to men, and we were capable, now, we knew, of even clearer thought than they, because we had ceased to believe the lies of sexual politics. We knew that a world without rape would be one in which we were seen for what we are, and we would grow as large in our powers as we were able.

And when I ask how did we come to envision a world without rape, I am asking about the shape of revolutions because when one dreams of a new world, this world immediately becomes possible.

II

To believe something about oneself (or of others that one has power over) is to help to make it true. There are studies which show that a teacher's expectations of a student's intelligence are usually met with the degree of intelligence expected. Hence this movement of disbelief, in which women formed a kind of mental energy wave and began to unburden ourselves of any notion that we liked suffering or oppression, was a radical act, a transforming act. Even the act of naming our suffering as oppression transformed us. The more we believed we did not like suffering, the less we found suffering, of the sort that is inflicted on one being by another, tolerable. We allowed our anger over the infliction of pain to be expressed and in that expression found more of the truth of our feelings.

I am aware that this is a classic form of knowledge, that it is the path of many therapies and healing, and also of the processes of writing and art. Creation. One allows. One follows feelings. They open and reveal deeper feeling and finally deeper meaning, and finally at some point those meanings began to transform and transmute.

This transformation moved many of us away from the political movements we had before followed. I had been a part of the student Left. From Marxism I had learned a habit of looking for social causes and observing how human nature is shaped by external condition. I named other atrocities and broke down other silences. What I learned from the movement for Black Liberation—the right to speak for oneself, the right to rage at the infliction of suffering— permeated my very soul.

But that Left had an ideology, which, beyond and in addition to its prejudice against women, did not agree with the changes we experienced. The strictly Marxist and socialist part of the left insisted that history moves only through class conflict, and since women are not a class by that definition, our efficacy as social changers became *sui generis* negligible. We were, in short, not important. This, of course, sounded like an echo to us of what we had heard all our lives.

In their rhetoric, the issue of rape, which seemed to be central to us—at the core of something which we could not fully explain, perhaps our being—was an epiphenomenon, a spin-off several generations away from the real cause, which was division of labor. And just as rape as a real and altogether too palpable phenomenon was diminished in their minds, so was it diminished in their agendas. Rape, after all, would only go away when capitalism did. The only real act hinged on the organization of labor. But this did not ease the burden which rape had put on our spirits, to organize labor.

We rejected the theory that capitalism had raped us. If they said patriarchy was just a form of capitalism, we said that capitalism was a form of patriarchy. But our departure from these old ways took place on a far deeper level than this dialogue. There were other leftist theories from which we departed, but our most serious difference was that theory had ceased to impress us as much as it had. Experience had become more important.*

---

* By this I do not mean to argue against thought or scholarship but rather to question the separation between thought, feeling and experience. Among other things, this separation ultimately leads to authoritarianism, and to the worship of certain theories for their own sake.

In our actions we went right to the sorest wounds. The stories we heard of women who, after being raped, were hounded by the police in a kind of inquisition as if the woman had provoked the rape, created a terrible pain in us. We moved to act there, to stop the bleeding there. After numerous speak-outs were held, in which women stood up and told of having been raped, and then abused by the police and the judicial system, after giving ourselves the so desperately needed time to speak about a long hidden injury, we worked to change these more outrageous injustices inflicted on us by the very system which claimed to protect us.

Perhaps there was a wonderful logic in these moves that we did not see then. The traditional political left often calls such moves *reform*. In truth, changing the procedures of the judicial system does not stop rape. Still the logic was there, clear, brilliant with that kind of certainty that only emotional logic can have. True, rape itself is intolerable. But there are degrees of intolerability in the mind and these have to do with justice, and justice with the mind itself. Susan Sontag so accurately calls morality the realm of the imagination. And it is in the realm of the imagination that some of the greatest agonies are suffered; if I imagine myself guilty, even though I am not, I suffer as if I were.

And this precisely is the devastation that a legal system and a police procedure which questions the victim as if she were a criminal inflicts. If she accepts that indictment against herself for the violence done to her, she must feel guilt, and a guilt weighted with centuries of hatred for the bodies and sexual feelings of women. If, on the other hand, she does not accept this guilt, she suffers a sense of powerless outrage. Injustice of this order, that authority should blame the one who has been violated, can tear one apart. Especially if there is no one to hear or see this particular crime, or to affirm that injustice has taken place.

Hence a body of listeners and seers became, as part of our movement, an institution. We created rape protection centers. Women sat and listened as another woman who had just been raped told her story. *She was heard.* And this was healing of a festering wound, even to those of us who had never been raped, because such is the nature of a community or a movement. We all suffer what the others do in our minds.

And so we have centers for the care of rape victims and in many places police procedures have been changed. In other places, they are changing. (And in many places the old wrongs are repeated.) And then we moved also to change the courtroom procedures and the laws. That old practice whereby the woman who was raped was scrutinized in the courtroom, the history of her personal relationships brought in as evidence that she was not in essence rapable, was changed because of the feminist movement in many states.*

So too was the cautionary instruction of the judge removed, his direction to look at the victim's words with special suspicion, as if women are more liable to falsify, especially regarding sexual experience. And the legal requirement for corroboration in cases involving rape was also removed, so that, like a victim of robbery, or mugging, evidence from the one who was violated is all that is needed now in many courtrooms.

There *were* changes: the laws changed; courtroom procedures changed; police procedures changed. Still, and here we might fall under the shadow of defeat and say, nothing has really changed, and even feel somehow as I *have* felt, even if these conditions are not natural like earthquakes or tornadoes, even if rape is an unnatural occurrence, the truth is, the force of society is too great, the force of habit too deep; rape goes on despite our struggles.

For look at the statistics. (Statistics again—this is always a bad sign, a kind of failing of the heart, I think, when we need statistics, but yet bear with me.) The statistics say that from 1972 to 1976 rape has increased by 105 percent. How we ought to read this is not immediately clear. No crime involving violence to a human being has increased faster. Yes, of course, we have other considerations to take into account here. Perhaps the feminist movement, in removing the shame for many women in the fact of having been raped, has actually caused the increase of the number of reported rapes. Yet again, by the same logic, since this movement has also made it memorably clear that going to the police and then sitting through a trial can be a harrowing experience for a woman—almost as bad, sometimes worse than the rape itself—it could be said that fewer rapes are being reported.

We can ask a second question of the statistics though. Are there

*For a more thoroughgoing discussion of the change in rape laws by one who has worked long and hard in this effort, see Camille LeGrand, "Rape and Rape Laws: Sexism in Society and Law," *California Law Review,* 1973, 919–941.

more convictions? But even if the answer to that is yes—except that it is not yes—but even if it were we still must ask again how many rapes out of the many are actually reported, and then we must ask how many rapists are caught. The statistics themselves on all these questions don't give us a very hopeful picture, but even if they did, would we believe them? The truth to us, in our daily experience, is quite different.

In Berkeley, where I live, the streets have gotten more and more dangerous. Staying in one's own house is risky. There is a man who has been raping women in this city for half a decade. Still he has not been caught, and when one hears that he has moved into one's neighborhood a kind of atmosphere of fear starts to permeate the sidewalks and the trees outside the windows. And he is not the only one. We know this from the way we have to protect ourselves; violence against women is growing, not diminishing.

The old theory would tell us this is a failure, only material change is real, reform is a compromise, believe that shadow of defeat.

But now, as equally and strongly as I know, without statistics, that violence against women continues, I also know we have not failed; we are not defeated. I do not *feel* defeated. This is what comes back upon me whenever that shadow falls of defeat, thinking we have not yet stopped rape, I do not feel defeat.

And now I search and reach for why. In the first place, I cite to you Carolyn Craven, one of many women who was raped by this man in Berkeley. She happened to be a reporter, a very well known one because a very good one. (And indeed let me say here, because later the relevance will be more clear, the fact that she was a reporter on public television had *everything* to do with a feminist movement for liberation and a black movement for liberation, both of which demanded people of our kind represented among newscasters.) And how can I tell you what it felt like to hear Carolyn Craven speak out about this rape. A kind of opening of the field. This terror, this subjection, this humiliation and torture, she said, we will not bear. I remember him, she said. I hold this man accountable. I hold this city accountable. I do not bear this act alone. We do not. We do not accept this state of being of submission and trembling and fear for our lives, of locking the door against brutality and sleeping uneasily, of our lives on edge, we do not accept this.

This in itself is such a healing. Imagine, those of you born after this movement began to make its mark, and remember, those of you who are older, what it was like before, when a reign of terror fell over the women of a city because a man was going about doing violence. Because no one then spoke out in anger and rage, no one said this is not right, this will not be. A horrible disheartening silence covered the whole affair, and each woman suffered her own fear privately and in this fear also suffered the private and unholy shame of those women who happened to be attacked. I tell you that in such an atmosphere it is truly hard to breathe.

Now, the materialist in me, and there *is* one, speaks up here and says, yes, yes, all this is true but this is not enough. No, I answer, no it is not. The whole strength and beauty of Carolyn Craven's speaking out and our speaking out is that none of us feels that the matter ends here. *We are saying the matter is intolerable.*

The change we have wrought is a change in consciousness. The actual condition of rape continues, as do all the conditions of women's lives which cannot be separated from rape. Through manifested acts, woven inextricably into the dominant culture, the idea of woman as a diminished being still rings through patriarchal society. She who must work longer hours and harder for less, she who is beaten and hounded by her husband into fear and hiding, she whose body is tortured in the public imagination in the name of pleasure, she who has no power in her own government, whose voice is rarely heard— this is the being who is still raped.

The atrocities continue, and we have not yet even named them all. Only two years ago, in 1976, the first International Tribunal of Crimes Against Women was held. Forced sterilization, clitoridectomy, denial of birth control, persecution of lesbians, brutality toward women giving birth, economic exploitation, these continue all over the world. And yet the conference began with these words, not defeated words, but words of overcoming, of movement.

> Strengthened by your solidarity, you will develop defensive tactics, the first being precisely the one you will be using during these five days: talk to one another, talk to the world, bring to light the shameful truths that half of humanity is trying to cover up. The Tribunal is in itself a feat. It heralds more to come.

In itself a feat. It heralds more to come. I want to mine these words which Simone de Beauvoir sent to the tribunal, to find meanings perhaps even past what they were intended to mean, because this is where we are now, in time. This is what we have.

Yes, we do not yet have the end of rape. All we have is the feat of naming rape a crime against us. But how could changing police procedures and law bring an end to the raping of women? We have just said that rape is not isolated from the whole condition of women which remains a diminished condition (except now in our minds). The miseducation of young girl children, the complacency with which mutilating operations on female bodies are accepted, the poverty of women and children, that any woman anywhere feels she is not beautiful or is too old or is not fully human—all of these cause rape. They cause this act slowly, and through subtle turnings, but still certainly and predictably. When we confront rape, suddenly a whole system becomes visible, a system which includes invisibility and silence, which had covered the crime of rape in silence, and of which silencing and the ignorance of our history of protesting our condition has been an active part. So it follows that rape does not end with the changing of laws; that the causes go deeper and belong to the whole fabric.

And did we ever believe in the first place that these little changes would take away the whole crime? Did we, for instance, have a Grand Plan, in which the changing of laws or setting up of centers for the protection of women was simply a First Step? A part of a program? No. Our decision to set up places where women could be looked after by other women was not made out of revolutionary theory. In all our acts, there has been a voice heralding more to come. This is a passionate voice, a voice which has given to our small, seemingly hardly significant changes an excitement, a joy, beyond what rationally one might consider belongs. But this voice did not proceed from theory. This was a voice intrinsic to and birthed from what we did. And what we did was always, and still is, to heal ourselves.

We did not move from theory; we moved quite simply, as I wrote before, to the sorest wounds, and in this sense, we were no longer "thinking" in the way that Western man thinks, in the realm where thought is divided from feeling, and objectivity is imagined to exist. We were discovering a different sense of clarity, one achieved through feeling, in which thought followed a direction determined by pain, and trauma, and compassion and outrage. This is why we made these places where women who had been brutalized might be cared for.

Yet these small changes in the doing of things were in themselves a feat. And they do herald more to come. Because the making of these small changes changed us. And these changes inside us were not small; we were profoundly different now than we had been before.

There is an old trick known by doctors of the mind and even some of the body, and most nurses, and certainly any woman who has had the care of the ailing. Any little change for the better is liable to start a whole process in motion, and especially if that change is begun by the patient herself. Belief that one is getting well is in itself curative for the ill. To comb one's hair, brush one's teeth, stretch, to attend to even the most irrelevant detail can cause a more essential turning, go into cells themselves it seems, wake up in the body a desire to breathe. No textbook, no objective medical analysis, can tell what that detail might be which releases. An old, accomplished nurse often has hands which know to guide her patient to her own resources. This kind of knowledge is called intuitive and it is called feminine.

There is a saying which is part of Oriental medicine and that is that Ki, or energy, or the life force, follows mind. Placing one's mind and heart in a certain direction, believing, can make it so. Certainly many women found this to be true when they learned to defend themselves. Much of the study of martial arts, besides the physical development of grace and skill, is a change in attitude. To work against fear, shock, a feeling of defeat. To use the energy of the attacker against himself. And this change in attitude brings about a change in the material. The body becomes stronger, quicker, gravitates to the physical, seeks movement; and the body which feels strong, which feels it can defend itself affects the mind, cannot be seized in the same way by fear, transforms the psyche. In this way, no change we experienced was simply itself but made other changes. And the shape of each change became a lesson for us in possibility.

We did not lack sophistication. We knew we were supposed to have theories. Indeed, the presence of this goal, to change the whole order of things, was an issue among us. We lived in a mood of vigilance and still do that our movement not end in a series of ameliorating social services.

We were not satisfied that women had gotten the vote, just as we knew the women with vision in the nineteenth and early twentieth century who had struggled for that vote had not intended for the matter to end with that accomplishment. We would not be satisfied if the centers we invented for the caring of women who had been raped got sucked up into officialdom, standardized, bureaucratized. In this, what we were doing would be lost as surely as certain artifacts, certain sacred objects, lose their meaning utterly in even the most careful replicas.

What was it in what we did that could not be replicated by this social order we try to see ourselves past? On a very practical level, we went about things differently than they are usually done. Writing of the parallel movement to set up women's health care centers, a woman in Switzerland warns, "They must not become imitations of already established institutions by, for instance, being seduced by profit, having a hierarchy of salaries and workers, and by practicing established medicine."

Really, what happened that was so radically changing for so many of us, was that, as we began to create our own places (and this includes places of the mind), everything fell under question. None of the old ways of thinking and doing were assumed to be right.

This was not an easy way of being. We struggled among each other, sometimes gloomily. We had to discover that creating our own lives was not an answer in itself, but only a beginning. Paradise is not conferred on the liberated. We became free in these places of our own creation only to see troubles and failures of our own making.

But our failures have been pale beside what we have wrought within ourselves. Can we begin to see this now when the future to so many seems portentous with violence and scarcity?

Helen Marieskind, writing of the self-help clinic movement says,

> The self-help clinic and the women's health movement are not just personal solutions for an individual women's health problem—though that is obviously a valid reason for their existence: they are tools for inducing collective thought and action from which radical social change can grow.

But let us look closely at these words. To begin with, to say that a clinic might validly exist as a solution for an individual woman's health problem is a radical statement! If women are suffering in our bodies, this suffering should be met. This suffering should not be tolerated. Most really revolutionary change seems, after the fact, to be self-evident. That all children should be educated. That workers ought to receive enough pay for a decent standard of living. That it should be a crime to enslave another human being. These are all self-evident to us, but what a labor it was to bring this evidence before a self which civilization had damaged and contorted into thinking otherwise.

In assuming that women's bodies ought to be cared for we are pushing aside centuries of hatred for the female body. Of the malignment of women's complaints. We are challenging the belief that women ought to suffer, that physical pain is a part of our destiny and ill health a part of our biology.

But Helen Marieskind's sentence goes on and becomes more radical. She speaks of that motion where the patient begans to care for herself. These are our health care centers. We are directing the motions. We have initiated their very existence.

One must know the history of women and medicine to comprehend the depth of this change, and it is part of this feminist movement, part of the heralding more to come, that we have revived this history. I cannot tell the whole story here. A few details will have to suffice. For instance, the fact that midwives, who had been delivering infants successfully for centuries were stopped from practicing by patriarchal law. That the women burned as witches were often herbal healers if not midwives. That women were denied entrance for centuries into medical colleges. And that those who gained knowledge otherwise were refused the license which would allow them to practice. That most powerfully affirming act, to heal oneself, or, in the imagination to see oneself as having the power of healing because one knows that is part of being human which is being female, this is what has been denied us. And this and no less than this is what we have taken back when we have created health centers and centers for the care of women who have been raped.

Finally Marieskind says that these movements induce "collective thought and action from which radical change can grow." But how could they not? When one takes one's own healing which is to take one's own life into one's own hands, how can this not change our behavior and how we think and how we feel? *In itself a feat. It heralds more to come.* Healing, and the belief we can heal ourselves, and desire to heal and the decision to move toward healing are all radical acts which transform us in and of themselves. Once so transformed by these seemingly small acts, we are capable of vision, of imagination and more decisions and more actions, because by the process of caring for ourselves, we become more and more ourselves.

A woman is raped. A rape is attempted on a small girl. A woman reads about a rape in the newspaper. This woman does not report the rape to the police because the man who raped her was once a lover. The little girl is questioned rigorously by a policeman who wants to know if she makes up stories. The woman reading the newspaper sees the word *alleged* appear again and again in front of the word *rape.*

What would happen if these two women and the little girl met, if they spoke, if they were able to speak out what they felt to each other? What would happen if they discovered the same rape, the same hurt, the same feeling of being distrusted, perhaps turned into distrust of the self, suffocation from buried feeling, the same relief at finally knowing that what they knew to be true both in their own souls and in the world outside them was true. What happens when thinking and feeling beings begin to trust themselves, their own perceptions, *their own desires even?* What happens when we follow what we feel, do what we desire? If one woman holds another after she has been raped. Stays with her through the night. Listens to her story. If a group of women demand that a judge not caution his jury to distrust the words of women. Doesn't this same miracle happen when a woman knows, because her hands themselves have discovered this, that she can care for her own body, that she may know more than the doctor knows, because she feels. These are kinds of healing, to restore sight and hearing, to restore voice and movement, all through belief, because through these experiences, we believe ourselves again and therefore, we become ourselves as never before.

These new beings which we always were but had been separated from, these new souls never settle for the old ways which had buried them. And these souls can suddenly imagine more than rape centers, or laws changed, or even prisons full of men who have raped women. These souls, because they have had a taste of being whole, a taste of wellness, begin to desire even more. Now we desire a world in which rape could not be imagined and could never be. We desire nothing less than this.

What I have described here is a new shape for revolutions, though perhaps this is the way deep change has always occurred. Because the beginning is in feeling, and one follows the heart, not the head.

After all, our heads have been schooled in the old way of doing things, whether we call that way patriarchy or capitalism or tradition or the establishment, this is how we have been schooled. The right way of doing things. The way it has always been done. What the authorities say should happen, whether those authorities be Keynes or Marx or Weber or St. Paul.

About four years ago, I had a dream which was set at a radical political convention. I found a group of people whose ideas charmed me. I found myself sympathetic and began to march with them until I asked them their name. They said they were Trotskyists. What faction they were, in the dream, did not bother me. However, I was horrified to learn that they had named themselves after one man. My dream soul found this the height of absurdity, and I began to laugh in astonishment.

What we are schooled to believe ought to happen is always a rigidity, a limitation on what can be. As a poet, I have known this for years. When I begin to write, if I have in my head a notion of what the poem must be, the poem is always curiously, sadly, small and predictable. But if I follow the words which come from my feeling, often times not even knowing quite what they mean, certainly not guessing the outcome, I find the poem becoming wondrously large. My own words become a kind of gift to me.

Must not a real revolution transform even the expectations of the revolutionaries? And must it not therefore proceed, with all sureness, from the heart?

III

> Look at the skeleton children
> advancing against us
> beneath their faces there is no sunlight
> no darkness
> no heart remains
> no legends
> to bring them back as women
> into their bodies at dawn.
> —Audre Lorde, "Chain"

Whatever divided us from our own hearts so that we should even have to speak of such a thing as moving from our hearts, as if this were not natural? Where is it we have been? What strange life have we been living? These are the questions I awaken with in 1978. I find myself remaking myself each day, learning like a small child such simple things as where is the earth, where is the sky, what does my body feel like, how can I let my own weight give me grace, how do I speak directly, see, what does the world tell me, from moment to moment. Because I have been a damaged being, as we are all damaged. The real sources of my own power and knowledge were taken from me painfully, slowly and surely, as a child, as we were all so maimed in our sense of the real.

I discovered my rage and fear at the existence of rape. And beyond this? Solitude. Myself. What am I if I exist unprotected in the world? These are beginning to be questions for the soul, and these are the questions, after seven years of political questioning, which like the kernel of wheat after it has been held up to the wind, remain. But is this not what we have meant all along when we have demanded to be human?

And yet, we who were the objects, the "other," less than human, have found in our struggle to free ourselves from this less-than-whole definition which patriarchy lent to us, that no one in the patriarchy is fully human, that even what is called human in that world of dominance is sadly, deeply diminished.

Look what we discovered in our political motions to liberate ourselves from the terror of rape. We found all acts of transformation transform us. That we must follow our feelings; that we can heal ourselves; that we find the unexpected. But these are all words that concern the spirit, and yet the spirit has either a corrupted place in patriarchal politics, or no place at all.

In 1971, when I wrote the first part of this work, I considered the spiritual movement to be a digression, an escape from the real causes of human suffering. This was an attitude I had inherited from the Left, and which was natural to me at that time, since what I had known of the spiritual was mostly a hypocritical wielding of symbols in the use of power. As Nelle Morton has written of the official sanctity,

> The Lordship of Christ often becomes strangely identified with earthly lords and rulers who supply funds for certain religious groups to exist, invite its leaders to the White House, and use them to bless proceedings in courts and legislative assemblies.

When the spiritual was not divided from the political this seemed a sinister, almost sickening encroachment on liberty. And Marx's words that "all progress of the spirit had thus far been progress against the mass of mankind, driving it into an ever more dehumanized situation," seemed manifestly true, not only in the history of the atrocities of the crusades and the missionaries, but also in the history of the oppression of women, the burning of witches, and the long and virulent tradition of the hatred of women by the Church Fathers which supported those burnings and lived long after. In my own life, I ascribed many kinds of suffering, both in the body and the mind, to Christian ideas which had become part of me.

And yet in 1978 I find myself speaking with my own soul. And so I want to go back, further back into the reaches of the past and know where or how what was called spiritual became a way through which we were even further alienated from ourselves. Because now the old patriarchal habit of dividing one thing from another—matter from spirit, body from soul, the left hand from the right, the one from the other—no longer works for me, and I, together with many women in this continuing movement into our lives, find that things spiritual and things political are no longer separate.

I am trying in these pages, to tell how this happened. But this is not easy. I grope; the language is not available. What is here is old language with old connotations. Even the words *soul* and *spirit* have become so corrupted, so removed from immediate experience, mystified, used as mystification, as a way to alienate a being from herself. So I must just string together a series of simple stories and observations and hope this way we will find some thread of meaning.

First, I go back again to the matter of consciousness, consciousness which has become so significant to the feminist, and was so diminished for the Marxist. But in this there is a wonderful paradox. It was a Marxist education which in the first place made me distrust all theory and give experience primacy. But this is what led me, and all of us I believe, to consciousness and then to the soul—because we were more vitally interested in our own experience than theory. Where our experience contradicted traditional radical thought, we left that thought behind. And in our very living, in our paying attention to our real lives, we encountered the crucial fact of the significance of our minds, in no experience more dramatically than in the experience of rape.

In their statement against rape delivered at the International Tribunal on Crimes Against Women, a group of French women said this:

> Legally, rape is recognized as a crime with physical aspects only; namely the penetration of the vagina by the penis against the will of the victim. In effect however, the real crime is the annihilation by the man of the woman as a human being.

One physical act is not equal to another physical act. Rape is not a matter of spiritless atoms penetrating other dead matter. Mind comes to play. Will comes to play. The act is informed by centuries of the hatred of women, by a tradition of violence and fear toward our bodies, by St. Paul's words that we ought to keep silent, by the old rule that we must cover our heads in church. This is what makes rape a qualitatively different act than assault, or robbery. In both cases, one is forced, one is injured. But in the case of rape, the very odor of the body of the rapist, his gestures of brutality, the menace of his threats echo back into centuries of debasement and his penetration penetrates the very soul of his victim with, as the French women wrote, annihilation.

But isn't the thought that women have no soul one of the preconditions of rape, and is not rape, after all, a ritualistic playing out of that belief? Two monks in the fourteenth century wrote that women are not to be trusted in the realm of the spiritual, that this is why they are more open to possession by the devil. After the death by suicide of a film actress, another actress publicly declares, "They treat us like meat," by which she means that the men who hire them treat them as less than human, as matter without spirit. A young man who has committed a rape confesses that, as he forced this young woman, a stranger to him, her cries of fear made him realize suddenly, as if this had never before occurred to him, that she was a human being.

This is perhaps the most mutilating of dichotomies in these centuries, that some are seen as fully human and some are not. Simone de Beauvoir has written about us,

> Now, what peculiarly signalizes the situation of woman is that she—a free and autonomous being like all human creatures—nevertheless finds herself living in a world where men compel her to assume the status of the other.

This is also true of people of color, of homosexuals. The Other takes many shapes. And the mutilation which occurs in this act of consciousness through which the soul of the Other is stolen, is a mutilation which cuts both ways. For certainly it is mutilating to deprive the Other of a soul, and beyond a doubt it is mutilating to rape. No wonder indeed that the spirit has a doubtful life in the patriarchy.

But this may be the reason, finally, that our very selfish motion, to heal ourselves, to tend to our own wounds, may turn out to be the most radical motion of all, one that heals not only ourselves but eventually all, and thus transforms the social order absolutely. For indeed, the rapist does not feel the agony of rape; the nature of his particular mutilation is a numbing. To fail to see the soul of another is to truncate perception utterly. But the one who is raped cannot rest still with her situation. She is turned on a rack, herself and her own body put in direct opposition to the state of the world as society has asked her to accept it. Of this de Beauvoir writes,

> The drama of woman lies in this conflict between the fundamental aspirations of every subject (ego)—who always regards the self as the essential—and the compulsions of a situation in which she is inessential.

How could a woman be more quintessentially inessential except when she is being raped? Her very life is under threat of extinction. The dictates of her soul are rendered without effect. And any sense of being essential in this context must therefore be an extremity, an act which strikes at the core of patriarchy. Isn't this the reason why under the law it has been so much more acceptable for a man to strike out against the rapist of his wife or his daughter than it is for the woman herself to do so? Behind the letter of the law is a reasoning based on property rights, so that even here the crime of rape is not a crime against an inessential being but against her owner, the essential being who is her husband or her father.

Was not this the real question behind the trials of Inez Garcia, Joanne Little, Yvonne Wanrow, and now Dessie Woods?* And how significant really that these four women are all defined as the inessential Other in two ways, both as women and as women who are of another race. How can the Other have the basically human right to defend herself against violence? Her life is not essential.

Indeed, to find in ourselves that quality of being essential is no

---

* Each of these women was put on trial for murder because they killed the men who raped them or, in the case of Yvonne Wanrow, also threatened her children.

small task. This process does not stop with eliminating shame at being raped, though this is a beginning. We must strip ourselves to the very core, strip away all the patriarchal learning, the old alienating definition of soul as not female. I find it significant that Inez Garcia decided to protest her case publicly when she heard of the rape of two girl children. When my daughter was born, I suddenly felt a new level of rage at what had been done to women, what is done to us, from birth. It is as if we must somehow be able to imagine ourselves as innocent and new born again if we are to reach within ourselves our own essentialness.

And essence, after all, is another word for soul, is another word for spirit—the spirit which is lost to the rapist and the raped, in this transgression. And so there is a shape here after all, moving from the political to the spiritual.

But there is more. The motion has even more of a shape, winds in more intricate patterns, yields more details. There are other stories. Because the stripping away which one must do in this patriarchy to retrieve oneself goes on in many ways. And one of them was in the realm of traditional religion itself. For alongside protests against rape and the poverty of women and the many material ways of our brutalization, steadily, over these last seven years, women have been retrieving what was lost to us in culture. There were a multitude of starting points. The use of the word *human* to mean "male." The use of the term *him* to mean "her" and "him", but still always really "him". All the books by women fallen out of print, not taught to us in school; paintings by women stored away in museums; female mythology subtly changed over centuries so that what was female became male and the very features by which we recognize the heroic became masculine. That God is male. All the ways our presence has been erased from the mirror of culture. Another aspect of our non-being.

And so we began to reprieve pictures of ourselves. We wrote, sang, painted. We recovered the writings and markings of women who lived before. We scrutinized all the old stories and images handed down to us so that we might gaze directly on the hatred of women in these tales. The story of Lilith. The story of Eve. The paintings of Salome and of the Madonna. And in all this we found two amazing revelations which may be keys to this rejoining of the spiritual and the political I attempt here.

One of these revelations was that the patriarchal religion was not only incidentally misogynist but that hatred of the female (and with that the uncontrolled, the emotional, the intuitive, the dark, the world) is woven so inextricably into these religions that one might say this is *the* hidden content of, for instance, Christianity. And at the same time we discovered another revelation: that there were, at different times in history, different religions and mythologies which worshipped female gods.

To place before one's mind the image of a Goddess. Not the goddess as consort or mother or younger sister, but as the powerful one, the source, the revealer of mystery: If a woman is to become essential, must not this image be a possibility for her?

And then, of course, the actual shape of history began to suggest more. Nothing could be proven absolutely. What we had, what we have, are suggestions. But that is all we need. We remake the past in our minds, for now that is all the past is for us anyway—a place in our minds which has its greatest power in perhaps determining for us what we can imagine as the future.

We received the suggestion that those women who were burned by the Christian Fathers as witches were indeed the priestesses of a different religion, one which was more female not only in its offices, but in the more transcendent meanings of the word female: closer to the earth, listening to natural spirits, emotional, sexual, dark. We recovered images from prehistory. Rounded female Goddesses, found buried in fields, left from older civilizations. A Goddess with snakes as symbols of power wound about her arms. The sacred calf. The tree of life. The symbols which the patriarchal religion had called evil.

And indeed we found that in this mythological world the story of rape was told with great clarity. That the sites of matriarchal temples, such as Knossos on Crete, were chosen because the surrounding hills made the shape of a female body. That a female deity preceded Zeus. That Zeus raped Hera. And then we listened with new ears to the story of the rape of Persephone—how the daughter was stolen from her mother, how she was raped with her father's blessings, how her mother made the earth unyielding in revenge and received her daughter back only by compromise.

All this knowledge worked a kind of alchemy in us which cannot easily be described by rational means. Can I say simply that a woman who can perceive in herself the Goddess cannot so easily be shamed by rape? That she is more likely to shame her rapist? For we are not protesting anymore that we too are human. We are not bent and strained to argue that we do not want rape, eager to prove that rape is a crime. We take our essentialness as self-evident now, and our work begins with this. So we begin to see, and we see differently. We see what is not there. We see visions. We know there *is* a world without rape and this world is in our minds.

IV

> *When you have buried us   told your story*
> *ours does not end   we stream*
> *into the unfinished   the unbegun*
> *the possible*
>   —Adrienne Rich, "Phantasia For Elvira Shatayev"

We are essential. We are translucent to ourselves. We have taken the power outside us within us. We have stripped away the voice of the authority. We become our own authority. We are the only ones who can say if we have souls, and we say we do, and these souls speak to us. Our conversations with the spirit are our own. No one else translates, or listens in, or can tell us what has transpired. What we know we know. We speak directly to the spirit.

And was this not Anne Hutchinson's crime? In the sixteenth century Anne Hutchinson was banished from the Massachusetts Bay Colony because she preached, and because of *what* she preached. In trial, when she asked why she should not preach, Governor Winthrop and the elders of Boston quoted to her the words of St. Paul, "I permit not a woman to teach." When the Other stands up and acts as if she is essential, this act by itself challenges the existing order.

And yet again, Anne Hutchinson, having had the experience of the Other, must have had that consciousness, undergone that old stripping away somewhere in herself, redefined the world, been born as new outside the old definitions. What she preached tells us this must have been so. Even in the angry and condemning words of Governor Winthrop the luminescence of her vision comes through. She taught, he reports, a covenant of grace as opposed to a covenant of works. What grace meant in that time and ethos and that community was that one knew God only directly through an immediate revelation of the spirit, and could not be said to be saved because of regular church attendance, or wealth,* or any baptisms conferred by earthly authorities. This idea clearly moved Winthrop to terror. He wrote, "Many good soules, that had been of long approved godlinesse were brought to renounce all the work of grace in them, and wait for this immediate revelation."

But how exciting these words sound to me. How much I desire that "long approved godlinesse" should be thoroughly renounced in me. How I value this "immediate revelation" for which I wait, and which I receive, and for which I wait again daily. And yet how dangerous is this idea, this theology in which the soul speaks directly to the soul and her universe.

And have we not then, in the stripping away of the voices of patriarchal authority from our minds in order to make ourselves essential once again, established for ourselves a direct relation with our own hearts, our spirit which is the same as the universe, the spirit?

Consider just this. The same voice of patriarchal authority which declared that women desire pain and ought to cover our heads in church is that which eventually separated things political from things spiritual, matter from soul, and declared all that was not material as unreal. Science now replaces the Church Fathers with its own religion of atheism. Patriarchy has judged its own god as dead. And this is most certainly true. Those who rape have murdered their own souls. But we who have been the raped are not enclosed in this system. We are inessential only to it. Not to ourselves. And our souls

---

* From a materialist point of view, or to one concerned with circumstances and social conditions, belief in the covenant of grace might appear to be a reactionary theology, since participation in the mystery of grace does not necessitate any outwardly caring behavior toward others in order to achieve salvation. Yet in the context of seventeenth-century politics the covenant of good works was in fact the more conservative theology, since it ultimately bolstered both the authority of the church and the Protestant work ethic. In its more developed and extreme form, this covenant acted as an apologia for the rich; wealth was said to be a sign of internal holiness. Of the question of caring, I remind myself that Anne Hutchinson was a healer (she was a midwife). And to this apparent contradiction I bring the Buddhist idea of compassion, that is, of a spontaneous act of warmth which because it is creative, is also propitious and deeply kind, but which never springs from the calculated desire to be charitable, "good," or religiously correct. I imagine a true state of grace would generate this kind of compassion. And here too I remember these lines from H.D.'s "The Flowering of the Rod," "I go to the things I love with no thought of duty or pity."

then, once we step outside of this enclosure, are not dead. Neither is the spirit of the world, we can see now, dead.

Knowing this, should it be a surprise that the feminist movement has led many of us to speak directly, and now I am being concrete and particular, with spirits. I myself have found a new way of being in this world.

I know that hands find the places on the body which need touching. Certain places have become sacred for me, as if the trees there have held part of my soul and know me. A light falls around the body, a light that can touch and be touched and flows from one being to another. One tree grieves for me when I am sad and is glad to see me when I visit. The day I suddenly wanted so deeply to resolve a long bitterness with an old friend that I saw her clearly in my mind's eye, she appeared a few moments later before me in the flesh. And deer come to me and linger at those particular moments when my own nature seems to crack and open to me so that I speak directly with the universe. I call to an old friend who is dead; I say, give me a sign of your presence and in the next block her name appears over a storefront I have never seen before. I stare into the mirror at the bones of my face, I stare into the charred hollow of a tree trunk, at another women's hands. I touch the skull of a deer, touch the place between my breasts. Around the objects carved and revered by Eskimos, I can feel a presence. After playing music here I begin to feel a presence in the air outside my kitchen. Because I share a kind of bread with a friend in love, this bread is forever filled with her, evokes tenderness in me, comforts me. Gradually my whole landscape *is* touched, is sacred. Day by day I shed the old rational apparatus. I become more and more alienated from the assumed way of thinking and doing, but—and this is the miracle which keeps me in this direction—I become more and more myself, less and less alienated from that self for whom, more and more, I feel a great love.

Can I say here how wild I feel? That the visions in my mind are as real as this manifested vision of the patriarchy whose streets I must negotiate every day. How is it I can let you know that this is becoming daily more true for other women all over the country. And that we find new powers in ourselves. New ways of hearing and seeing and healing. That we begin to feel a kinship with the ways people thought and think in tribes, in Indian cultures. That we feel the universe speaks to us, cares for us, leads us. That what we experience directly from the universe finally has more power for us than what all the authorities of "approved godlinesse"—the doctors, the scientists, the Academies—have taught us.

This then is how finally, in 1978 when I turn to write about rape, I decide to write about how this violence impinges on a woman's spiritual life. In the nineteenth century Susan B. Anthony, the political leader, and Annie Besant, the spiritual leader, could not agree. They thought their worlds, the spiritual and the political, to be separate. Now we erase this old, damaging separation. Now women all over speak of the spirit in political language, of the political through the words of the spirit. Mary Daly, once a Catholic theologian, creates an image of what has been called God—this being at the heart of things—which cannot be a noun, must be a verb, a process, a becoming, our becoming. Nelle Morton, another feminist, imagines "a great ear at the heart of the universe hearing human beings to speech—to new creation. A speech that is human speech—human word—my word and your word. Our word become flesh."

Our word become flesh. We are inside ourselves. We have felt ourselves as never before. I tell you this and offer no evidence except the words on the page because no evidence of such an experience can be given. Except to know that we are learning to love the essence in ourselves, and thus we learn to love each other in ways before unimaginable.

V

> *Now we are ready*
> *and each of us knows it   I have never loved*
> *like this   I have never seen*
> *my own forces so taken up and shared*
> *and given back*
> *After the long training   the early sieges*
> *we are moving almost effortlessly in our love*
>　　　　　—Adrienne Rich, "Phantasia for Elvira Shatayev"

1978. I go deep into myself. I suffer the pains of the past which I know I have always carried with me. I see that what I saw before as real was delusion. Every motion I make to heal myself widens my vision. This comes upon me as joy, as an experience of gladness, that the world can be what I imagine. Rape is an invention. Rape can be unimaginable. I feel this is my very flesh, this flesh which opens to joy. I feel safety. I know what this state is. I feel blessedness. I say we can pronounce this world differently. Our word can become, flesh.

PART 3

Consciousness
1978

I

SOLITUDE. THE MIND'S eye dreaming. The child unwatched. In her room, assuming voices. Afternoon light low through a grove of oak trees: light wind, silence, a small animal in the underbrush. The continuous dialogue. Lakes become sorrow reflected; the sea washes away the inessential. Oneself honed to the core, finally, reaching quiet.

"To destroy the phenomenal world and regain the unconditioned," Mircea Eliade writes of mystical experience, one must "withdraw to the center of oneself." The phenomenal world, in the consciousness of women, in the years since 1971, loomed large; our work was to name conditions which as part of the obscurity of women's actual lives, were before this time, unnamed. We spoke of rape, as we did of abortion, of our economic deprivation, even as we named oppression as a state we knew, prejudice an event from which we suffered. The rhythms of hunger and the needs and crises of children, the dominating requirements of houses, all the bodily needs of families, all the conditions women face daily—this was our traditional work. But in these years, these phenomena widened also, in the minds of women, and we began to see the cares and work of women as social too. Still, these conditions have not changed, and in these years, while I was raising one daughter alone in an economy and society hostile to our needs, I, as many women must, longed for "the unconditioned." But despite our political work, the "unconditioned" was not palpable.

Yet language too is a condition which can determine our behavior as surely as the physical, and language did change. We named. And this naming rent a hole in the way we had been seeing. We *remembered*. And the one I found in my memory was a girl. A girl who loved to be alone in the woods, never worried about grass stains, or wet earth, whose spirit was moved there to see beyond the phenomenal because, when she was alone, she *withdrew to the center of herself*.

And now, eight years after writing of rape and thus naming that actuality to myself, when I return to this subject, the word *solitude* comes to my mouth, and I know I must speak of the fear of rape and what this does to the solitude of women.

All the little girls who were menaced in their solitary journeys— Little Red Riding Hood, Goldilocks—the woods being the place where Snow White could be found if the woodsman had wanted to cut out her heart, and the woods being the place where the bodies of children, most often girls, were found, changed somehow, according to the dark reports, after their abduction. The images. The film that begins in the apartment where a woman had lived alone. Signs of violence. Police standing about. The woman's parents, staring into her dead face, "We begged her not to leave home!" A woman driving alone on the road, stops at a roadside inn, a motel, and in her room, in her shower, is stabbed to death. And is there an echo to the words, "Do not walk here alone at night; do not come to this place unescorted," an echo from a time we cannot remember, but still must sense, as all human history lives in the present in seemingly mysterious signs: the words of the witchburners who said, "When a woman thinks alone, she thinks evil." *

I have been told often not to go into the woods alone. One day I saw a small figure who was watching me on the hill opposite and across the valley. Could he see that I was a woman? I could see that he was a man. But he turned. Moved up the hill and out of sight. Still halfway across the valley I went into a grove of trees which I

* Heinrich Kramer and James Sprenger. *Malleus Maleficarum*. trans. Mortague Summers. (Arrow Books, 1971) London, p. 115 (citing Seneca).

felt covered my presence, and waited. Whatever I had come into that valley to work on in my mind was erased now by this struggle. I tried to forget that I had seen him watching me, but I could not. He stayed in my mind even as I called myself foolish to hide, to suppose any danger. Then, as I reached the other side, he appeared suddenly on the path before me. I dropped back, let him walk ahead, waited until, if he had kept on walking, he would be out of sight again. But some sense, a sense that women all have from years of living with this fear, made me go out to the very edge of the path to where I could see around the undulating hill and know for certain he was gone. He was not. He was sitting just behind a curve, just where I would see him only when I was upon him. Now I knew terror. We were half a mile away from the entrance of the park. This was solitude. I grasped some rocks and some sticks and ran by another trail, so that I came out ahead of him on the path. He had started walking, but I was running with a lead and ran the whole distance out of the woods to my car. I waited to confront him, but he must have chosen not to try and overtake me. And so I tried to forget the fear. I went home to work and worked for hours and did forget, forgot so thoroughly, that the incident did not come to my mind, when, at night, I emerged from my study, tired, strangely uneasy in the dark house, and fearsomely lonely. I did not know how I had become such an abandoned creature, cold, and a stranger.

II

> *Might suffered at the hands of another is as much a tyranny over the soul as extreme hunger ... when food means life or death. And its empire is as cold, and as hard as though exercised by lifeless matter. The man who finds himself everywhere the most feeble of his fellows is as lonely in the heart of a city, or more lonely, than anyone can be who is lost in the middle of a desert.*
> —Simone Weil, "The Iliad, Poem of Might"

How does one begin to write about loneliness? One circles the heart of it, describes what is absent. A reassuring presence is not there. Everyone knows loneliness and the battle we meet there. The child must learn that she is separate and that the reassuring presence of her mother can go and can return. Of this genesis of feeling, Lillian Smith writes,

> But though we can never quite put the feeling into words, anxiety is not made of mysterious stuff. It is as much of the essence of earthy human experience as is tenderness. Both are feelings that begin to grow during the infant's prolonged helplessness; both are nourished on those inseparable needs of a child to be taken care of and to be related to a human world. Then, it is, when we are so long at the mercy of the Mothering Ones, that we learn our private definitions of tenderness, and loneliness; of sympathy, and terror; in intimacy, and isolation.

And because the need to be taken care of, to survive as a vulnerable creature on the earth, and the need to be related, to love and be loved, are inseparable, in loneliness are encapsulated both the experience of rejection and the fear of death. But how simple the link between rape and loneliness! Aloneness becomes loneliness when one is afraid for one's survival, *endangered*. And of love? But rape, which is a violent attack, must come from hatred. I have always imagined this act as emanating from hatred, a hatred of me, even though the rapist does not know me. Can one's relation to the world be more severely ruptured than by a hatred for oneself by an enemy who does not know one? To be unknown and hated.

And this linkage reaches further. At the same time that she sees there is an "I" who is different from her mother, and from the other, the world, the child begins to perceive herself both as a being and a cause, a force, in the world. She tries to control the comings and goings of her mother. Her life is shaped by the attempt to bring love and caring when she would will them. And finally, as part of this trial, she begins to locate badness in herself. She can be bad, she imagines, she can lose affection because of her badness. *I am left because I am bad*, she says. And isolation is a kind of punishment: the child's room, the prison, solitary. Thus, the rejected reject themselves.

That a grown woman, alone at night, may see herself as rejected, not part of a couple, not chosen, and therefore unworthy, bad in the sense of not good enough, is an evident part of our culture. Yet, when to this rejection is added the intrinsic statement that she is not good enough to be protected (from the violence of rape), and when to this is added a second statement intrinsic to the fact of rape, *someone wishes you harm, someone hates you*, and when to this again is added the old primal fear of death which is part of the threat which always accompanies rape—the weight of loneliness, its invidiousness to the self, can become unbearable.

Yet for the adult consciousness to ever fully experience itself, aloneness must become solitude. This is a hard passage for anyone, coming sometimes unwilled, like a gift, when, as Lillian Smith writes, the chasm between the self and others seems "so narrow that a mere plank would do on which to cross them." Then the world is a sympathetic place which one can enter and leave at will, and so one *wills* to be alone. And it is in this aloneness, Smith tells us, and we know, that one learns. There might be a small anxiety we begin to take with us there on the other side of the chasm, some minor disquiet, which in this quiet of ourselves we can remake, risking newness of perception, perhaps rebuilding or building a different bridge to the world. But the anxiety must be small, and the world a trusted place.

So, to learn aloneness and to begin the learning in aloneness, one must school oneself in trust and will a sympathetic universe into being. But how difficult the existence of rape in that universe makes this willing. Whenever we are alone, in the woods, on a deserted city street, in a house in the country, or an apartment, even in the empty places of some public buildings, we see terrifyingly wide chasms between ourselves and being, because we are in danger.

Solitude. To have this we must give up the sense of being abandoned and learn that the other has freedom of movement. A reassuring presence can leave a room with no cause from us. Our badness does not cause aloneness. We are not bad. Yet what if *someone wants to rape me, someone hates me*?

And of the fear of death itself? Is not one, after all, always alone in the moment of death, and must this not, finally, be accepted if aloneness itself is to be accepted and solitude achieved? Death is change. One loses control. One moves into the unknown. And again, to step into the unknown one must perceive the universe as sympathetic, trust, let go, assume benevolence, that this *is good*, this leap into what could be nothingness. And yet again rape transgresses our solitude. For what if this fear of death comes most often in the fear of being murdered? Murder. Death from malevolence, from hatred, from someone's desire *that I should not exist*.

Not only does someone hate me and want to rape me, but *someone wants me to die*. A knife, a gun, a closed fist, "Stay still, or I will make a jigsaw puzzle of you." The tender of prostitution is money; the tender of rape is violence and death.

We are frightened all of our lives by the incipience of this violence: The rapist may be a stranger, or a man we thought we knew. The act of rape for women is of its very nature never predictable, never *chosen*, never a fight one has wagered on, always a surprise attack, and for no reason. In the moment of rape a woman becomes anonymous. Like all victims of terrorism, there is something awesomely accidental about her fate. She is like the duck flying in formation which the hunter chose to shoot down—she appeared in his gunsight. Absorbed by his violence, her soul and the history of her soul are lost, are irrelevant.

III

> *And when our parents tucked us into bed and were safely hidden in the living room, we would pop out of bed like jack-in-boxes and dance with the shadows or furtively bring beneath the sheets our toyfriends and fantasies. Some nights it seemed that only the bear staring in the window or the ghost moving in the attic above could get us to be quiet.*
> —Mary M. Watkins, *Waking Dreams*

Yet for the child, nothing is ever irrelevant or lost, and that part of us which is child-like and still alive, accepts all experience with wonder and does not discriminate. So the intellect may say that rape is merely a casualty, a mistake, and irrelevant to one's soul, as the experience *is*. But the violence and hatred of the act do not feel irrelevant. The child's mind accepts this act as right and looks for a reason. What does the small girl feel when she is first told why she must be home before dark? What does she believe?

The list of admonitions we must give our daughters is long. Do not look into strange men's eyes. If they look into your eyes, look down, look away. Never talk with strange men or boys. Do not go into alleys, into dark unpopulated streets. Be home before dark. Never accept a ride. The world, even a girl's neighborhood, becomes a mined field.

I was not eager to create this field for my daughter. She must have heard hesitancy in every syllable I pronounced. I labored to let her trust the world. And she had just passed through the age of terrible fears of the dark, when her room was the haunt of grizzly bears and other monsters. These are necessary monsters, the analysts say. They are projections of fears, of anger, perhaps anger at the parent, or of the fear of retribution for small transgressions, or retribution for anger itself and rebellion. They come from the child's psychic struggles and float back upon her consciousness as foreign menaces. When she learns her anger will not destroy, that she cannot harm with her secret thoughts of violence, nor will the world harm her because of them, the bears and ghosts become faint and finally vanish. But that is about the age when a mother must tell her daughter that there are real monsters.

And why are these monsters displeased with her? They are displeased because she is turning from a child to a girl, from a girl to a woman. Like the overlooming and majestic atmosphere in Chinese painting, sexuality washes in the background to this threat to a child's or a woman's existence: our own sexual feeling. Can it be coincidental to these circumstances of our culture (because rape is a circumstance of our culture) that until the last decades, sexual feeling in women has been defined, *sui generis*, as bad? When the witch-burning Church Fathers wrote that women's thoughts, when alone, are evil, they meant this evil to be a sexual evil. "All witchcraft," they wrote in the same text, "comes from carnal lust, which in women is insatiable."

And what misogynist sexual morality waits in the studies done over and over to determine how often women provoke rape? Did she have sexual thoughts? A sexual crisis? Did her movements, her clothing, her assertiveness, her submission, her fear, her fearlessness reveal a desire to be raped? Behind these musings are the old prejudices that the sexual feelings of women are like sirens leading men to rash actions against their better selves, as if these feelings have in fact an inherent badness which naturally find their correlative in the world in male brutality. (The child's anger come back to haunt her again.) Does not the guilt of the one who is raped, that shame of the "victim" so often called irrational, or even priggish, does it not in this ancient woman-hating frame become reasonable? The monster is a fantasy. But if the monster becomes real, if the secret sexual life which has for centuries been called sinful is embodied and is menacing, then how eloquent is this affirmation of one's own evil.

These gestures seem so commonplace among women—we draw the window shades before undressing, pull a cloth quickly over the middle of our bodies, cross our arms over our breasts. Thus we imagine we protect men from themselves. The very existence of our bodies then, our own gestures say, is provocation to violence; our bodies become *things* which we must hide. How does one move about the world in this body which has the power to invoke malevolence against oneself?

Are not all our acts judged against this power of our bodies? There is a narrow pantheon of images inside which we are supposed to exist. These images have little to do with the living of our lives nor with the felt moments within us, and yet they ride over our experience and admonish us. They constrict our consideration of our own behavior, invading even our private thoughts, limiting our dreams, and the width that desire might be able to give to our imaginations. This power of our bodies is not the same as the power of being one can experience within oneself; this is a power which exists only in relation to male desire: the power to attract, the power to inspire desire, the power to allow or not allow. Thus the images in this pantheon are sadly limited to what pleases or does not please the male, the one who has power over us. There is the seductress, the *femme fatale*, the Lady of Camellias, the manipulatress who uses male desire. There is the frigid woman who does not use male desire (and ironically, the lesbian is cast into this circle, since her sexuality does not exist in relation to male pleasure). There is the good woman, the wife, the one who knows the true exchange value for her body. And finally there is the child-woman, the pure, whose innocence is a sign of stupidity, who believes she is liked for herself; she was "born yesterday," and the rape or ridicule she receives is a lesson for us all.

But what of our own desire? What of our experience of our bodies as we are inside ourselves, not as provocation but as being? This culture is a *cul-de-sac* for the power of women. Desire itself is seen as provocation. The professors seek to prove in their studies that women are raped because we want rape. Our own desire, which is inseparable from our power in the world, because desire must be the beginning of all action, becomes the harbinger of violence, the feelings in our bodies dangerous to our bodies, we enemies of ourselves, our badness to want, the monsters real.

And if we recover our desire, refuse these admonitions, reject the arguments this culture of rape makes against us, still we live with the fact of rape and the fact that men do see sexuality in women as an invitation to attack. And so this sexual impulse at the heart of our bodies which is the impulse outward and toward the world, a reflection and material of all feeling and thus wedded to our strength as animal creatures must be curbed in the body, even if not in the mind. And our bodies, learning the habit of careful deportment in public places, speak to us steadily and clearly, saying, *you are not free.*

Is it through this illogic and this logic that solitude in a woman's life becomes confinement? The sexual self is by definition solitary. One must be a solitary *being* to desire and move toward union with another. Yet confinement, which so often causes women to be alone, is not solitude. *To destroy the phenomenal world.* Because confinement is phenomenon. It is caused from the outside and is therefore alien to *the center of oneself*, the polar opposite of the unconditioned.

The phenomenon for instance of her children. She must stay home with the children. The confinement of her pregnancy. The confines of her labor. Her house. And the confinements of time in domestic labor (the hour of the infant's rising, the bedtime hour, mealtimes). And the rhythms of her mind defined by the continuous possibility of demand—interruption that is expected—and therefore, unlimited thought unimaginable to her. Her body, always answering to the needs of others, confined by an unnatural tiredness. Her body itself, which might in other circumstances be a touchstone, telling the way to what is real, in the culture of rape, becoming an enemy, and therefore also a confinement. She herself a prison.

"Range is masculine and confinement is feminine," Mary Ellmann writes of the stereotypical ethos. She quotes Freud's letter in which he states of his future wife, Martha Bernays, "I will make every effort to get her out of the competitive role into the quiet, undisturbed activity of my home," as an example of the Victorian sentimentalizing of the confinement of women as shelter.

And this "quiet, undisturbed activity" if it were willed, would sound like solitude perhaps, a kind of meditative space. But Ellmann draws another meaning from it. She invokes the word *practicality* as woman's sphere, a sphere not chosen, but enforced upon her by the same male world of power which has idealized her condition. "This is a forgivable limitation, Ellmann writes sardonically of this confining image, "as long as they shut their mouths and chill the beer. But unfortunately many tend to form and then to express narrow and hostile opinions of masculine projects, and some may even prevent their realization." Thus women, by providing the fire and food which make male creativity possible, because of this very confinement to practicality are depicted as too stupid to recognize male genius—as in the woman employed as a housemaid who was reported to have started a fire with Carlyle's manuscript of *The French Revolution*, or as in Nora Joyce's concern that her husband wasted paper. But Ellmann aims more at the heart of this deprivation when she writes,

> Even falling off a cliff, the mother thinks, Mother of Three Falls Off Cliff. And drowning, she cannot review her entire life as she should, her concern being entirely confined to the now forever unshaken unfolded beach towel on the beach.

The tragedy of such images is that we may take them into ourselves; we may become them; certainly our souls suffer from them. And at the essence of this image of woman as narrow and practical is such a severe lack of concern for her being, that indeed, in this view, her soul disappears.

Where can the soul of a woman go in this world? Outside her house is the phenomenon of rape, waiting to confirm her own evil, even to destroy her. And inside? All the phenomena of the needs of others. The value of her life is predicated on her service to others. (And this practical service, contingency, maintenance, what De Beauvoir calls "immanence," always the opposite of the creative—which even when directed toward the "other" is still an expression of self.) Her existence, ringed by an impersonal atmosphere of hatred, is, at its core, of no *intrinsic* value. Does she *have* a soul?

Patriarchy has insisted until the twentieth-century (when the question of souls has been deemed unscientific) that women do not have souls, or if we do, that they are small. This insistence is of itself a phenomenon—*you have no soul, your mind is limited, your world is trivial*—this voice a shaping influence. How well the voice of patriarchy echoes the phenomena which make it seem impossible for women to *regain the unconditioned*!

IV

Every woman's death diminishes me.
—Adrienne Rich, "From an Old House in America"

To regain the unconditioned. Mrs. Ramsey, a female character created out of the consciousness of female experience and genius (whose character was in fact based on the life of Virginia Woolf's mother, Julia Stephen), does have a soul, and in Woolf's *To the Lighthouse* she reaches through the conditions of traditional female life to touch upon it:

> Children never forget. For this reason, it was so important what one said, and what one did, and it was a relief when they went to bed. For now she need not think about anybody. She could be herself, by herself. And that was what now often she felt the need of—to think; well, not even to think. To be silent; to be alone. All the being and the doing, expansive, glittering, vocal, evaporated; and one shrunk, with a sense of solemnity, to being oneself, a wedge-shaped core of darkness, something invisible to others. . . . When life sank down for a moment, the range of experience seemed limitless.

"Not as oneself," finally she realizes in this meditation, "did one find ever, in her experience (she accomplished here something dextrous with her needles) but as a wedge of darkness. Losing personality, one lost the fret, the hurry, the stir . . ."

This observation is part of every religion: to gain serenity one must lose the outward self; to find the soul one must renounce the *ego.* And thus it has often been said of women, that because we deny ourselves, our needs, our egos, we are more spiritual.

Still, real instances of female spirituality are effaced from history, denied, or punished, and this common idea of the spirituality of female nature does not include the religion of those women who were burned at the stake as witches, nor is it really meant to include the voices of Joan of Arc, nor the mystical visions of St. Teresa of Avila, nor of Hildegarde von Bingem, nor the lives of medieval abbesses, nor beginners of the early Marian tradition, nor the female Christian mystics after the dicta of Paul. Because the patriarchal description of female experience does not assume the existence of a self through which to voyage to a communion with what is beyond the self, and women are never, in this spirituality, supposed to speak directly with the universe.

This is the sense in which women are supposed to be more spiritual than men, in the same sense that womanhood itself is by definition a renunciation in favor of men. The Catholic Church canonized Maria Goretti because, though she did not submitt willingly to rape, she refrained from attacking her attacker and forgave her murderer, renouncing her rage for charity. Women attend church. We light candles, we make certain, though it is men who read and are illumined by the texts, that religion exists in the home. Even our own spirituality must be renounced for others, because the *raison d'etre* of our souls is to save men.

So Dostoyevski's character Sonia Semyonovna discovers and saves Raskolnikov's soul. But her efforts are innocent of original thought (or at times one feels, any consciousness at all). Raskolnikov is the genius. Sonia has no answer to his super-rational questioning. She is nearly mute and can only read him the holy scriptures. Her persuasion is by example, and the example she offers is a selflessness, not born of, but shaped and sharpened by a steadfast and unwavering love for the genius. Her love is truly spiritual, and this in exclusion of bodily sensation. One feels, in the purity of her love for Raskolnikov, her body would get in the way. (And, after all, it is a soiled body.) And yet her example is not particularly to be followed by him. Rather it is the selflessness of her love which finally bears upon him, impresses him. And forgiveness and not passion is her real gift. Forgiveness is at the apex of her healing power. But what does she forgive? She forgives the murder (*Every woman's death diminishes me*) of another woman.

And what is Sonia Semyonovna's experience? In his introduction to the Vintage edition of *Crime and Punishment,* Ernest Simmons writes,

> It is a tribute to Dostoyevski's genius that he is able to breath the breath of real life into a character whose nature is so passive and submissive. Although she reminds one of an allegorical personification of some abstract virtue in a medieval morality play, Sonia transcends her allegorical significance through the sheer force of the novelist's art.

If the shape of this woman's experience is determined by the needs of the errant masculine soul to which she devoted herself, the feel of her experience is so faint that, were it not for masculine genius, one would not know it at all. Her experience scarcely exists.

Her experience is like the experience of Maria Goretti. After her death, the child affected the transformation of the man who raped and murdered her. He saw the light and afterwards devoted his life to serving a holy order of monks. But Maria Goretti, the agent of his miraculous experience, has no experience of her own. Her story is dominated by the story of *his* salvation. She is dead. And Sonia has none, for she does not have enough consciousness, or self, to experience. And yet that is the essence of the spiritual *experience*. And one must have a self, and an awareness of self, in order finally to strip it away, and know a deeper order of being.

How can one learn from the act of giving up what one has never possessed? Such a soul cannot be said to exist.

But Maria Goretti was a girl, not yet grown, and Sonia is a fiction, part of a pantheon of female virtues who are made to appear lifelike through "sheer force." In life, the movement is otherwise. Women are real, full of experience, and possessing soul; force works daily to rob us of self, of consciousness of self and of our souls.

V

In her essay, "The Iliad, Poem of Might," Simone Weil writes, "Might is that which makes a thing of anybody who comes under its sway. When exercised to the full, it makes a thing of man in the most literal sense, for it makes him a corpse."* Yet that is not the only sense in which force reduces, not the most common way that force acts, for it is the fear of violence, more than acts of might themselves, which reduces us to less than ourselves, daily. The question of tyranny, for the dead, is over. And for the living, tyranny manifests itself not so much through acts carried out as through acts threatened. In the same essay Weil writes,

> The might which kills outright is an elementary and coarse form of might. How much more varied in its device; how much more astonishing in its effects is that other which does not kill; or which delays killing. It

*For calling my attention to this essay by Simone Weil and its relevancy to these questions regarding rape I am indebted to Michele Cliff for her work in an unpublished paper, and for conversations with her on this subject.

must surely kill, or it will perhaps kill, or else it is only suspended above him whom it may at any moment destroy. This of all procedures turns a man to stone.

Or turns a woman to stone. For more than rape itself, the fear of rape permeates our lives. And what does one do, from day to day, with *this* experience, which is, after all, experience which denies experience, experience which says, without words and directly to the heart, *your experience, your existence, may end, at any moment*. Your experience may end, and the best defense against this is not to be, to deny being in the body, as a self; as we teach our daughters, to avert your gaze, make yourself, as a presence in this world, less felt.

How this less felt presence of women reverberates in the politics of sexuality! Politics is in its essence the relation between beings, the I and the thou, the one and the other. The same set of beings who define us as Other is the one who rapes us, or threatens us with rape and violence, and those are the same beings who govern us. Our governors threaten us daily with violence: we live under tyranny.

For the flavor of the fear of rape is not the same, for instance, as that fear the colonialist may feel when he confronts the terrorism of the guerilla. The guerilla is not his governor. He is the one who wields power over the guerilla, and though this terrorist may wish to reduce his governor to a thing, he cannot. Only the confluence of a threat to one's existence and power over how one conducts one's life can cause this unholy transformation.

"From the power to transform him into a thing by killing him there proceeds another power, and much more prodigious, that which makes a thing of him while he still lives," Weil writes. How do we tolerate this? But that toleration is a creation of tyranny. Weil continues,

> He is still living, he has a soul, yet he is a thing. A strange being is that thing which has a soul, and strange the state of that soul. Who knows how often during each instant it must torture and destroy itself in order to conform? The soul was not made to dwell in a thing; and when forced to it, there is no part of the soul but suffers violence.

To torture and destroy itself in order to conform—how well, as women, we know those words! How well we know this state of being, where being is not ours. And how much more subtle this second violence. For the first violence is undeniable. One sees the corpse. Who can dismiss the oppression of the maimed or murdered? But fear works a quieter course, less decipherable—like the threat from which violence proceeds, the marks are invisible, yet there and indelible, and choking all movement, for once we move from fear, terror accompanies every outward motion, and we are diminished.

So the position of women is identical to the vanquished, enslaved, and captured, of whom Weil writes in all respects except one. Not only our bodies, but our sexual selves are threatened, ringed with hatred, tyrannized. It is our sexuality which is the focus of the rapist and his wish to possess and humiliate. Sexual humiliation is the core of the act of rape. Eros. Attraction. Impulse toward. Adoration. Passion. These are powerful—the experience of these are powerful. So too must be the humiliation and denigration of these, the force against the willed force of these feelings.

This malevolent answer from the Other to one's sexual being sounds deeply in the body, and the threat of the act of rape is inherent in the dominance of men. How can women love men? Again Weil's words bear on us,

> On no occasion has the slave a right to express anything if not that which may please the master. This is why, if in so barren a life, a capacity to love should be born, this love could only be for the master. Every other way is barred to the gift of loving, just as for a horse hitched to a wagon, the reins and bridle bar all directions but one.

Women do love men. But how. In "The Maids," Jean Genet gives to one of the maids the line, "Slaves cannot love," and this in a drama which displays the hatred of the maids toward each other, and hence toward themselves. It is commonplace to say that love must come after self-love. Yet how can women, who have consented to be women, love ourselves? To consent to be a woman is to consent to renunciation of self. There is no one to love. To love or to be loved. The hitched passion must be something else, perhaps the desire to be like the master, or, love of power, or gratitude that she is not finally, murdered. Or perhaps passion will exist in any way possible, even though the stage for its enactment be the same stage on which female passion has been called evil and has met violence. This is the only place her passion is allowed to be.

Does this not illuminate the special sexual violence reserved for the woman who is, or who is perceived to be, a lesbian? Raped.

Beaten. Limbs broken. For men who love men, the police, and gangs of young men (looking for the effeminate to punish and brutalize in a man's body), must be feared. Women who love women must fear the violence, or the desired violence, of all men.

Like all real tyranny, there is no escape. A woman who recreates self love, and loves other women, is still living in a world shaped by the act of rape. A woman who loves a man who has chosen not to dominate, to disassociate himself from the power of rape, is still threatened by rape from other men. And yet, because we survive, and the soul emerges and reemerges and will not be quiet, we are proud. We do not, most of us, go about fearfully. This would give to the other even more power. We assert our dignity. We cannot be touched, we say to ourselves. We exist outside desecration and enslavement. So that when the act of rape becomes actual, even if we are not ashamed, even if we do not falsely imagine this act as an emblem of our evil, still some life in us crumbles. We have been made to recognize tyranny and what has been taken from us, made to see by force that we have become powerless. And this knowledge, even while it enrages, destroys.

So, finally, Iphigenia, so that she will not be destroyed chooses her own death, for if it were forced upon her, she would not die as herself.

VI

We who witness Iphigenia's death cannot accept it. The oracle has said to Agamemnon that he must sacrifice his daughter in order to go to war. In Euripedes, the struggle over this decision is played out by a man and a woman, Agamemnon, the girl's father, and Clytemnestra, her mother. The tension of the play is nearly unbearable; it is as if all existence cries out against this death, and yet, we know who will win because we know who has the power. All the action of the play has about it the odor of inevitability, not as a chance happening of blind fate, but as the predictable outcome of a system of dominance, the one over the other, that *is* blind.

So the death of the child must be preceded by a revelation of Clytemnestra's history at the hands of Agamemnon. We must know that she was taken by force into marriage. We must hear Agamem-

non, in another discussion, assert that his will is law, and hear Clytemnestra respond, with irony, "I have mastered the art of submission." We must know that the one has power over the other. And, in
his unlimited power, we must know of Agamemnon that he did not
stop at slaughtering the sacred animals to feed his armies; that he
knows the oracle to be false; that his war is waged not so much for
justice but for power and the domination of riches.

In these circumstances lie the seed of Iphigenia's death. But this
is also the death of Clytemnestra. In pleading for her daughter's life
she cries, "Don't make an evil woman of me", for this death, and her
recognition of her powerlessness to prevent it, must seal her to hatred.

But Agamemnon does not escape fate dictated by might either.
He, too, is turned to stone. Iphigenia, in asking for her own life, says
to her father that she wishes she had the voice of Orpheus that she
might be able to charm even the stones and thus win his love. It is
his love that would allow her to live. She is dependent on that. But
he has turned to stone. Had she the voice of Orpheus, a male voice,
she might charm even stone. But she is female; her voice has no such
power. Her state is the same as her mother's. "If you kill me, you
also kill her," she says and these words, together with Clytemnestra's plea, "Don't make an evil woman of me," reverberate through
the play. Iphigenia dies a physical death and thus becomes a thing;
Clytemnestra is reduced to an object while she lives, in Weil's
words, "a life that death has frozen long before extinguishing it."
Because, as Weil writes, "That a human being should be a thing is
from the point of view of logic, a contradiction; but when the impossible has become a reality, that contradiction is as a rent in the
soul."

As a rent in the soul. Such is the power of the phenomenal world
on the lives of women, and this is how cunning the *cul-de-sac* of our
situation is, that when we would shed this phenomenal world, and
draw deep to the center of ourselves so that we might regain the unconditioned, when we seek solitude, we are most in danger from this
phenomenal world. And is this not a religious problem? Before every
epiphany, and before each revelation or initiation into the sacred,
one must admit ignorance. One must be blank. Give up assumptions,
and shed ego, the daily self. Be prepared to leap into emptiness.

Emptiness. The dark. The abyss. The edge of death. Union and loss of self. Falling. The unknown depths. The void. The moment of transformation is a leap of faith. One trusts existence. Emptiness and the unknown, even in shapelessness, become benevolent. As Weil writes "something stronger than I was compelled me for the first time in my life to go down on my knees." But that something stronger must be felt as good, that which one wants to be part of, as the light, as the universe, not that which would reduce one to a thing.

Yet for women, the dark, deserted space, unknown geography is not safe. For us, *emptiness implies a malevolent presence*. And is it by accident that in the same mythos in which Iphigenia is sacrificed to her father's religion so that he might wage war, Zeus establishes his power first by raping his mother and then by raping his wife? Or that the king of gods has chained Hera by golden bracelets and anklets to chasten her for challenging his power? This same Zeus, as the father of Persephone, gave Hades his blessing for the abduction of his daughter into hell, while Demeter, her mother, suffers this rape as her own, this loss as a part of herself gone.

But one cannot say that the human father, Agamemnon, does not suffer his daughter's death. The play is a play about his choice; we watch the play of this decision on his psyche. "Such is the nature of might. Its power to transform a man into a thing is double and it cuts both ways; it petrifies differently but equally the souls of those who suffer it and of those who wield it." When one is the malevolent presence, emptiness becomes more than frightening; this void is hell. And in the act of experiencing might, to reduce another to a thing, the rapist suffers the consequences of the universe he has created and which he must then inhabit. This universe is ruled by might, and he himself is subject to it. The tyranny of might does not destroy his self, but rather constructs a self that is inimical to revelation. Revelation, after all, comes only through vulnerability, both in men and in women. The armored warrior cannot see. One must admit *one does not know,* one must give up control. If the imagined spirituality of women is false because it has derived from an absence of being rather than being, the spirituality of men is totally subjugated to the self of the phenomenal world. And hence has religion in patriarchy gotten a reputation for hypocrisy; the missionary precedes the imperialist; the holy fathers are greedy; religion is something which must be unmasked, because all it is is a mask. And like might, those on both sides of a mask suffer.

The religion of the fathers is part of the phenomenal world which one must destroy before regaining the unconditioned. And in the unconditioned, when the paradigms of patriarchy have been cast away, exist new vision, new possibility.

Once this phenomenal world is repudiated as the only real world, conditions which patriarchy has pronounced as natural or inevitable fall into a different light. All that which has been posed to us as scientific and objective truth, in this state, where we are withdrawn to the center of ourselves, can be questioned. In this light, the very way patriarchy sees loses force. The act of rape which embodes a denial of the existence of the other as a real being with a soul, has its analogue in a patriarchal consciousness, a view of the universe, which denies intelligence in that which is perceived. As Mary Daly writes in *Beyond God the Father,* "Widening of experience so pathologically reduced can come through encounter with another subject, an I who refuses to be an It."

To refuse to be an It. In this there is joy, whatever the phenomenal outcome.

But must phenomenon and spirit always be split, as if one were the enemy of the other? Do they not in the end always rejoin? At the end of the nineteenth century, Susan B. Anthony, the political leader, pleaded to Annie Besant, the spiritual leader,

> Annie—why don't you make that aura of yours do its gallivanting in this world, looking up the needs of the oppressed, and investigating the causes of present wrongs? Then you could reveal to us workers just what we should do to put things right, and we could be about it.

Annie Besant "sighed and said that life was short and aeons were long, and that while everyone would be perfected some time, it was useless to deal with individuals here." To which Susan B. Anthony exclaimed, "But Annie! We *are* here!"

We are here now, and we see, and there are things that we know. In the same motion with which we have denied the naturalness of the phenomena imposed upon us, we have discovered ourselves. Of this Mary Daly writes,

In the rising consciousness of women, power is experienced as the power of presence to ourselves and each other, as we affirm our own being against and beyond the alienated identity bestowed upon us within patriarchy.

And against and beyond this alienation, within our very beings whose presence is now powerful to us, we have found knowledge. This knowledge of how the phenomenal world might be must have been hidden within us for ages, for this is familiar and simple, and has that quality of certainty which separates vision from desire or belief. We *know* that a world without rape is possible. This world exists in our minds, exists even in some of our lives.

We know this as we know the feel of air in our lungs, irrefutably. And along with this, we know other things which make up the dimensions of this world. In this world, the lives of other beings are held as sacred, as is the life of the self. The body of woman is cherished. Desire in that body is loved, and the spirit in that body is visible and recognized in the smallest daily movements. This world is real to us because we have felt it in our bodies, and because of its beauty and healing presence, even the questions we have about the nature of this world take on for us as much reality as the phenomena which still confine.

Would not, we ask, the recognition of sacredness in the other, of the spirit in the other, and this cherishing of a woman's body need to spring from a whole weave that must also include a different notion of power; one that acknowledges the power in each being, but eschews power over another being as a lower order of behavior? Would not this weave have to include the erasing of the possibility of other kinds of cruelties for which rape might be a metaphor? Could theft of food from the mouths of children exist in this world, or any murder of body or soul? What kind of mind finds rape unimaginable?

What does the inside of my mouth feel like when even the memory of rape has vanished. And how is it then, walking into the night, the first steps into the sweet, safe, covering darkness? And where do these steps take us? Are there mysteries outside our windows which will be revealed to us when we know the air is safe there? Who are we when we are finally safe with our own kind? Our kind. And what of the silence when there is no more such cruelty even imaginable as rape, what is the softness like inside such a silence, such a solitude. I have a taste of it now; it brings me near tears. I know this world we see the edges of is real. And because we see this world, we can make it be.

And as I write these words, I can almost see the night outside my window transform. But I know too, setting these words here how real are the forces against us, those who cannot or will not imagine things differently. Those who in some contortion of their minds believe they need rape, and all that goes with rape, to exist in this world. But I know too the world has changed before and the seemingly unchangeable has become different. And if I am asked to be cynical because of facts and numbers and probabilities, or defeats or imperfections in our efforts to change, or because of weapons which can destroy the earth or time and space which grow too precious, I answer that what I feel, even in the face of all this, is a joy in the possibility I see. To think of that night as a safe and covering place! So if I choose hope over dread, it is not only that I prefer hope in my bones, which I do, but that I have tasted freedom from fear, a world we imagine, and this small taste means more to me than large fears. This then, is not so much a conviction of the inevitablity of the outcome, but a powerful feeling of being which is the knowledge that sustains me. We are, as Susan B. Anthony said, on this earth. *We are here.* This is *our* place, the place of our imaginings, the place of our lives.

We are here. In *this* world, while the act of rape reverberates around us, destroying the unconditioned, emptiness, the possible. But if the act of rape has had the power to sever the phenomenal from the unconditioned, to reduce souls to things, keep us from the centers of ourselves, from self, or make of religion a mask, we know another power, and because we exist, we can know this well; a power not a might, not exerted over another, and a knowledge not separated from ourselves or others. We know. We have the power of being no force can resist. *We are here.*

Susan Griffin
Berkeley, California, Spring 1978

PART 4

The Power of Consciousness

A Collage

compiled by Sandy Boucher and Susan Griffin

IN THIS COLLAGE, we have woven together words from the feminist movement, events from our recent history, and reflections from the patriarchy, both ancient and modern, about women, all bearing on the subject of rape and the power of consciousness to change our lives. This collection is necessarily partial and its weavings eccentric, but we trust it to ring back into the life of each reader, so that her own experience resonates with the stories, the statements made, the wisdom revealed in these documents. We ring the bell; the response is hers.

Sandy Boucher and Susan Griffin
Berkeley, California, Winter Solstice, 1978

In order that we stop being victims, we ourselves must take up the struggle against rape. Individually and collectively we can break the silence and make it no longer a taboo subject, or something shameful which weighs us down.

French witness. In Diana E. H. Russell and Nicole Van de Ven, (Eds.), *The Proceedings of the International Tribunal on Crimes Against Women,* 1976

Few Latinas could fail to believe Inez Garcia's inability to describe the experience of rape to the policemen who arrested her. We are painfully shy about our bodies and about sex. When she later complained of pains "down there" to a woman prison attendant, she was taken to a doctor who reportedly implied that Inez was upset, imagining things, and didn't examine her. . . .

We Latinas are not encouraged to be articulate about any part of our experience, much less about sexual abuse. . . .

In the courtroom she decided to defy the twin *macho* assumptions of Latin culture, that a woman belongs to a man; and that a woman dishonored by belonging to more than one man is herself at fault, as sinful as Eve. She defied the shameful silence with which women, especially Latinas, are supposed to treat their own sexual enslavement. I am grateful to her.

Maria del Drago, *Ms.*, May 1975

"You could have screamed—why did you suddenly lose your voice?"

His words sank deep and bitter within me. For, dominated by a feeling of shame, I believed them. I could not face him, could not be entirely honest and open about such things—it was too shocking, too shameful; I was not entirely conscious of their truth. I was too poisoned with shame and dishonesty about sex to face any situation clearly.

Agnes Smedley, *Daughter of Earth,* 1973

When the defiled female says, "That is the gentleman who raped me," we need corroboration. If her jaw is broken, for example, that is proof of force. Otherwise, how do we know she was raped? The difference between rape and romance is a very thin line.

N.Y. State Assemblyman Joseph F. Lisa, *Redbook,* September 1972

In Holland rape is a hidden problem. The police admit that rape exists, but when a woman comes to them to report a rape, the reaction is often that she has provoked it. Very often she is not treated seriously. That's why the group "Vrouwen tegen verkrachting" (Women against rape) started in Amsterdam in November '75. . . .

In the first month we opened our center, we got 150 phone calls
from women who had been raped or assaulted.

Dutch witness. In Diana E. H. Russell and Nicole Van de Ven (Eds.), *The
Proceedings of the International Tribunal on Crimes Against Women*,
1976

Mamie Carter said firmly, "If you look at the laws covering rape
you'll see they all stem from the property code. Now Almeta—at
sixty-five a woman is not considered of much value as property so
her rapist wasn't even indicted. And if she is black too she's not even
believed. The fact is, people feel sex is obscene with the old, but you
all read the tittering between the lines. The fourteen-year-old girl
was property not really damaged since her hymen was left intact, so
her rapist was allowed to plead to a lesser sentence.

June Arnold, *Sister Gin*, 1975

So determined were the Levites that a reverent regard for the pa-
ternity of children be developed that among them even violent rape
was equated with marriage, much as it was among the Indo-Europe-
an-controlled Assyrians. In Levite law, the rape of a virgin was hon-
ored as a declaration of ownership and brought about a forced marriage.

Merlin Stone, *When God Was a Woman*, 1976

If a damsel that is a virgin be betrothed unto an husband, and a
man find her in the city, and lie with her;
Then ye shall bring them both out unto the gate of that city, and
ye shall stone them with stones that they die; the damsel, because
she cried not, being in the city; and the man, because he hath humbled his neighbour's wife: so thou shalt put away evil from among
you.
But if a man find a betrothed damsel in the field, and the man
force her, and lie with her: then the man only that lay with her shall
die:
But unto the damsel thou shalt do nothing; there is in the damsel
no sin worthy of death: for as when a man riseth against his neighbour, and slayeth him, even so is this matter:
For he found her in the field, and the betrothed damsel cried, and
there was none to save her.

If a man find a damsel that is a virgin, which is not betrothed, and lay hold on her, and lie with her, and they be found;

Then the man that lay with her shall give unto the damsel's father fifty shekels of silver, and she shall be his wife; because he hath humbled her, he may not put her away all his days.
Deuteronomy 22:23–29

The interviewer: Do you see rape as much worse than physical assault, or do you see it as equivalent?

Ms. Gold: I see rape as being worse in that it doesn't come from a need for money and it doesn't come from total insanity either. Whatever it is that causes someone to hit someone else is horrifying in a different kind of way. Rape seems to be so imbedded in our society. It seems just a natural outcome of the way that men are. And that is a really frightening thing.
Diana E. H. Russell, *The Politics of Rape: The Victim's Perspective*, 1975

Allowing a male friend into your home who turns violent and rapes you cannot be prosecuted in court. In the eyes of the court, allowing the male into your home implies consent for him to have sexual intercourse with you. The courts apparently see that opening your front door to a man means that the vagina is opened to his penis. As brash and boorish as these conclusions may sound, we must understand that they constitute the thinking of society and the courts, not of women.
Kathy Barry, in *Stop Rape* (pamphlet), 1972

People in Scandinavia have a reputation for being free and tolerant. According to criminologists, Scandinavian police are considered the least corrupt in the Western world. Nevertheless, if a woman has trespassed just a few steps outside the limited sphere of her accepted premises, she will be met by suspicion if she accuses anyone of raping her, or she will be downright disbelieved. If Scandinavian women really behaved as the liberated women people in many countries think we are, we could not count on being respected and treated with dignity.
In Diana E. H. Russell and Nicole Van de Ven (Eds.), *The Proceedings of the International Tribunal on Crimes Against Women*, 1976

Rape is a punishment without crime or guilt—at least not subjective guilt. It is punishment, rather, for the *objective* crime of female-

ness. That is why it is indiscriminate. It is primarily a lesson for the whole class of women—a strange lesson, in that it does not teach a form of behavior which will save women from it. *Rape teaches instead the objective, innate, and unchanging subordination of women relative to men.*
>   Barbara Mherof and Pamela Kearon, *Notes from the Third Year: Women's Liberation*, 1972

There is not real affliction unless the event which has gripped and uprooted a life attacks it, directly or indirectly, in all its parts, social, psychological, and physical. . . . Affliction causes God to be absent for a time, more absent than a dead man, more absent than light in the utter darkness of a cell. A kind of horror submerges the whole soul. During this absence there is nothing to love. . . . That is why those who plunge men into affliction before they are prepared to receive it are killers of souls.
>   Simone Weil, *The Simone Weil Reader*, 1977

The souls of women are so small
That some believe they've none at all.
>   Samuel Butler, *Selections from Notebooks*, 1950

I was raped by my father's best friend when I was 14. My father had died only a little time before this. This situation was really traumatic for me, not solely because of the rape, but mainly because it was the outcome of the rejection I felt by my parents and the lack of love which existed in our family. Afterwards, I was made to feel dreadfully guilty. This man blamed me. The next morning he told me I was a bitch, a whore, a little slut, etc., etc. And when I tried to talk about it, when I tried to say what had happened to me, people threw the same accusations at me. . . . Since I felt so completely put down at that time, I felt I had no choice but physical death or internal death. For years I suffered terribly because of this experience. I was 18 before I managed to speak about it again.
>   French witness. In Diana E. H. Russell and Nicole Van de Ven (Eds.), *The Proceedings of the International Tribunal on Crimes Against Women*, 1976

The atmosphere outside the [sorority] houses is less protected. "Hey, horny, over here," some fraternity boys yell at us as we walk across the street. At another house, there is a commotion on the roof. Four frat boys are checking us out and flashing numbers on cardboard from one to ten, judging our comparative assets. All the rushees make a supreme effort not to notice. . . .

It isn't over, not yet—there is still the so-called "pig run."

We girls traditionally pick up our bids—invitations to join a house—and then go running and squealing down frat row to our new homes—at least that's the chauvinistic fraternity version. Hundreds of frat men line the sidewalks on Saturday morning guzzling beer and hooting. . . . Last year, [a young man] tells me, one frat rented a 600-pound hog and brought it to pig run on a leash. It had a sign written on its back that said, "Where's my bid?"

Amy Linn, San Francisco *Chronicle*, October 2, 1978

I grabbed her from behind, and turned her around and pushed her against the wall. I'm six foot four . . . I weighed about two hundred and forty pounds at this time, and she didn't have much chance to get away from me. She tried. I pulled her back and hit her several times in the face quite hard, and she stopped resisting and she said, "All right, just don't hurt me." And I think when she said that . . . all of a sudden a thought came into my head: My God, this is a human being. . . .

It was difficult for me at that time to even admit that when I was talking to a woman, I was dealing with a human being, because, if you read men's magazines, you hear about your stereo, your car, your chick. . . .

Man who attempted rape at age 17, *Ms.*, December 1972

The childhood of women must be free and untrammeled. The girl must be allowed to romp and play, climb, skate and swim; her clothing must be more like that of the boy—strong, loose-fitting garments, thick boots, etc., that she may be out at all times and enter freely into all kinds of sports. Teach her to go alone, by night and day, if need be, on the lonely highway, or through the busy streets of the crowded metropolis. The manner in which all courage and self-reliance is educated *out* of the girl, her path portrayed with many dangers and difficulties that never exist, is melancholy indeed. Better, far, suffer occasional insults or die outright, than live the life of a *coward,* or never move without a protector. The best protector any woman can have . . . is *courage.*

Elizabeth Cady Stanton. In Gerda Lerner, *The Female Experience: An American Documentary,* 1977

If you wear a bikini or tiny miniskirt to the market, be warned: You are a neon sign asking for trouble.

Today's teen-age girls, with their freedom of dress, youthful trust, and heightened awareness of femininity are particularly choice targets for the sex criminal.

Marla Zellerbach, San Francisco *Chronicle,* June 8, 1970

To be gazed at is one danger; to be manhandled is another. Women as a rule are unfamiliar with violence, they have not been through the tussles of childhood and youth as have men; and now the girl is laid hold of, swept away in a bodily struggle in which the man is the stronger. She is no longer free to dream, to delay, to maneuver: she is in his power, at his disposal. . . . It is not uncommon for the young girl's first experience to be a real rape and for the man to act in an odiously brutal manner; in the country and wherever manners are rough, it often happens that—half consenting, half revolted—the young peasant girl loses her virginity in some ditch, in shame and fear.

Simone de Beauvoir, *The Second Sex,* 1957

I was trained to be numb, I was born to be numbered and pegged,
I was bred and conditioned to passivity, like a milk cow.
Waking is the sharpest pain I have ever known.
Every barrier that goes down takes part of my flesh,
Leaving me bloody. How can I live wide open?

Marge Piercy, "What Is Most Hoped for and Most Feared in the Matter: Judgement," *To Be of Use,* 1973

The sexual abuse of children, who are overwhelmingly female, by sexual offenders, who are overwhelmingly male adults, is part and parcel of the male dominated society which overtly and covertly subjugates women.

Florence Rush. In Noreen Connell and Cassandra Wilson (Eds.), *Rape: The First Sourcebook for Women,* 1974

Lowering her head, she begins walking slowly along under the cliffs. "He's not going to drive me away!" she decides, and shoves her fists deep into the pockets of her jacket. But already the knowledge of his presence has slid like a screen between her and her sur-

roundings. Thoughts rise in her like garbage from the bottom of a pond—sights she would rather forget, stories told by women in the coffee room at work, by her other friends. And she thinks of children. At what young age will a girl child hear that husky, whispered "Hey . . . look!" and turn to see the man in the darkened doorway, the man back among the trees, the man in the window.
>   Sandy Boucher, "Charm School," *True to Life Adventure Stories,* 1978

With regard to rape in marriage, the law in Portugal states that marital relations have to be maintained. The expression, "He used me," is the usual way rape in marriage is expressed in Portugal. . . . The husband seems to be able to use his wife's body in any way he wishes—to force her to have an abortion she does not want, to have her sterilized, to lock her up, or to beat her.
>   Portuguese witness. In Diana E. H. Russell and Nicole Van de Ven (Eds.), *The Proceedings of the International Tribunal on Crimes Against Women,* 1976

Woman's body *is* the woman.
>   Ambrose Bierce, *Collected Works 1910-1912*

We say our personal problems are political and should have political solutions. In consciousness-raising meetings, we go around in a circle speaking in turn. This is very helpful in giving each member a chance to compose herself and her thoughts. . . . The more concrete, specific, and personal the group can be, the more information it will have to work with. This body of experience will lead to your own feminist politics.
>   Noreen Connell and Cassandra Wilson (Eds.), *Rape: The First Sourcebook for Women,* 1974

I have gone through both these debilitating experiences, these attacks on my personhood, which rape really is, and yet I am standing here, and I am able to talk to you about this.
>   Danish witness. In Diana E. H. Russell and Nicole Van de Ven (Eds.), *Proceedings of the International Tribunal on Crimes Against Women,* 1976

I am a woman come to speak for you.
I am a woman speaking for us all
From the tongue of dust and fire

From the bowl of bitter smoke.
This is a song for strength and power.
  Meridel LeSueur, "Hush, My Little Grandmother," *Rites of Ancient Ripening,* 1975

There was a time when you were not a slave, remember that. You walked alone, full of laughter, you bathed barebellied. You say you have lost all recollection of it, remember . . . you say there are no words to describe it, you say it does not exist. But remember. Make an effort to remember. Or, failing that, invent.
  Monique Wittig, *Les Guerilleres,* 1971

"I'd kill a rapist if he tried to force me to submit to his advances," declares Erin Sullivan, a member of NOW.

Erin is not alone in her sentiment.

Recently, members of a group called Women for a Free Future addressed the Berkeley City Council on the subject of rape.

Erin dramatized the session by coming in at the end dressed in black and carrying an unloaded Winchester rifle. She had checked to see if it was legal to carry an unconcealed, unloaded rifle, and it was.

The women from Berkeley feel that they are representative of women all over the world who refuse to put up with rape any more. Among their demands from the Berkeley City Council were that free public transportation be given all women from dusk to dawn, that more streetlights be added . . . that self-defense be taught to female children in the school system and that women be allowed to carry loaded concealed weapons.

Meanwhile a check has disclosed that karate and judo classes in almost every major city are jammed. "I feel a lot safer now that I know karate," one student says. Other karate learners say that their rages go so deep that actually—at times—they fantasize about killing a rapist.
  Susan Berman, San Francisco *Examiner/Chronicle,* January 17, 1971

Entrance into radical feminist consciousness implies an awareness that the women's revolution is the "final cause" (pun intended), in the radical sense that it is the cause which can move the other causes. It is the catalyst which can bring about real change, since it is the rising up of the universally and primordially objectified "Other," discrediting the myths which legitimate rapism.

Mary Daly, *Quest,* Spring 1975

Rape Speak-out in New York City, 1971

New York Radical Feminists, Rape Conference, New York City, April 17, 1971

Women Organized Against Rape (24-hour crisis center), Philadelphia, 1971

Women in three blocks of Venice's North Beach organized early in September to combat rape in their neighborhood. Women exchanged personal experiences with harrassment and shared effective methods of self-protection. Women from Los Angeles Rape Crisis Hotline demonstrated self-defense techniques, and suggested such necessary safety measures as dead-bolt locks. A phone tree was organized so neighborhood women would be able to contact each other. The women planned a second meeting to learn more self-defense techniques and to organize other Venice neighborhoods.

Sister, October/November 1977

As part of their prevention efforts, some rape squads have adopted near-vigilante tactics. In East Lansing, Mich., members of the rape crisis center are said to have scrawled "rapist" on a suspect's car, spray-painted the word in red across a front porch, and made late-night warning telephone calls. In Los Angeles, the squad has adopted a counterharassing strategy: When a woman called to complain that a neighbor followed her whenever she went out, squad members followed the follower for three days. That was enough to make him change his ways.

Time, April 23, 1973

Dessie Woods has been in prison for more than two years now. On February 2, 1976, she was sentenced to a total of 22 years in one of the South's most notorious women's prisons in Hardwick, Georgia.

Since that time she has been the victim of brutal beatings, forced druggings, and nude solitary confinement. Her crime?

Dessie Woods dared to successfully fight back against one of the South's oldest traditions: White rape of black women! Her assailant, a white insurance salesman named Ronnie Horne, was killed with his own unlicensed gun, and, as it happens in so many cases, the victim, Dessie Woods, was made to be the criminal, and the dead would-be rapist was made to be the victim.

San Franciso Women's Center Newsletter, July 1978

New Smyrna Beach, Fla.: Two coeds were raped by a man armed with an ice pick but then turned on their assailant and strangled him to death with a scarf after he threatened to kill them . . . .

After reportedly subduing their attacker, the coeds went to a nearby farmhouse and called police. Police said the rape victims believed they had only rendered their attacker unconscious.

San Francisco *Examiner/Chronicle*, June 9, 1974

Thus when a white man rapes a black woman [JoAnne Little], the underlying meaning of this crime remains inaccessible if one is blind to the historical dimensions of the act. One must consider, for example, that a little more than a hundred years ago, there were few black women who did not have to endure humiliating and violent sexual attacks as an integral feature of the daily lives. Rape was the rule; immunity from rape the exception. . . .

There can be little speculation about the turn events would have taken had JoAnne Little been killed by Alligood. A verdict of "justifiable homicide" would have probably closed the books on such a case.

But she had the courage to fend off her assailant. The price of her resistance was a new threat of death, this time issuing from the government of North Carolina.

Angela Davis, *Ms.*, June 1975

San Francisco (UPI): The State Supreme Court Wednesday publicly censured S.F. Superior Court Judge Bernard B. Glickfeld for referring to a rape victim "in an insulting and inexcusable manner."

It was only the second time such judicial discipline has been used by the court. The other case involved Santa Clara County Superior Court Judge Gerald Chargin who was censured for racial remarks about Mexican-Americans.

Daily Californian (Berkeley), January 21, 1971

"We don't want a dyke in our commons," three men reportedly told a woman student at Ohio State University. "If you don't (move out), we'll show you what men are like."

A week later, according to the *YIPster Times,* they demonstrated their maleness to her by beating and raping her, successfully eluding an all-woman defense squad organized to protect her as soon as she had been threatened.

Rape has since become a major issue at OSU, with a "Demonstration of Outrage" by the local Women Against Rape, with a refusal by University Officials to take action other than expressing "concern for the safety" of all students, and with campus police saying they could do nothing because the victim feared retaliation and harassment.

Ammi Bar On of WAR described the shrubs, barriers, and high brick walls of the OSU North dormitory complex as a danger to women. She is helping to recruit and train women marshals for the campus. WAR is also calling attention to the antigay and misogynist attitudes of some male students and hangers-on around the campus. Students were asked to report harassment or gossip about any woman's sexuality to forestall any future attack.
Majority Report, December 10–21, 1977

In 1974 the Ohio legislature passed a law allowing damage suits by victims against rapists. The law has just been tested in a Cleveland court, and a woman was awarded $22,000.
Majority Report, October 15–28, 1977

Although societal attitudes no doubt are responsible for the present construction of rape laws, it is also true that this construction serves to reinforce those attitudes. If the laws were changed to relate more rationally to the reality of the crime and to the goal of sexual equality, attitudes about the crime might also change.
Camille E. LeGrand, *California Law Review,* 1973, *61*

Workshop on Rape, sponsored by San Jose NOW, April 29, 1973, issued "Recommendations for Revision of Rape Laws."

Women's Litigation Unit of San Francisco Neighborhood Legal Assistance Foundation, June 22, 1973, issued "Proposed Amendments of the Rape Laws."

In order to place the phenomenon of rape in its legal context, it is also necessary to understand the conceptual framework in which rape laws exist. Here the focal question is "Who or what do rape laws protect?" Legal writers analyzing rape laws have concluded that rape laws protect male interests: Rape laws bolster, and in turn are bolstered by, "a masculine pride in the exclusive possession of a sexual object"; they focus a male's aggression, based on fear of losing his sexual partner, against rapists rather than against innocent competitors; rape laws help protect the male from any "decrease in the 'value' of his sexual 'possession,'" which results from forcible violation. However accurate these conclusions are, it is interesting that these analyses have not focused on a woman's physical integrity, peace of mind, or freedom of movement without fear of sexual attack as fundamental values to be protected by rape laws.
Camille E. LeGrand, *California Law Review*, 1973, *61*

Women's Rights Brainstorming Group of American Civil Liberties Union of Northern California, All-Day Rape Meeting, July 17, 1973.

Sacramento: SB 1678, introduced by Senator Alan Robbins, D-Van Nuys, would limit substantially the instances when a rape victim could be questioned about her previous sexual relationships.
Berkeley Gazette, June 13, 1974

[Yvonne] Wanrow, a resident of Colville, Washington, was convicted of second-degree murder last year and sentenced to serve two 20-year prison terms for the admitted 1972 shooting of a convicted rapist, William Wesler. Wanrow claimed the man had threatened both her and her three children.

In an unprecedented move last year, the Washington Supreme Court, however, set aside Wanrow's first conviction and ordered a new trial for the Native American woman. The court stated that "In our society women suffer from a conspicuous lack of access to, training in, and the means of developing those skills necessary to effectively repel a male attack without resorting to the use of deadly weapons." Wanrow had argued that she used a gun on Wesler because she was in a cast at the time, and could not defend herself.
Plexus, July 1977

When Liz Bunding, a white belt in karate, yelled "Eeeeeeccccccccchhhhh!" yesterday afternoon, you could tell she meant it.

It was the women's liberation protest outside the second meeting of a male-only karate class in Harmon Gymnasium at the University of California at Berkeley.

And the ladies, 75 of them, were protesting the ban on females in the class with a karate demonstration of their own. . . . "Women need karate as a means of self-defense," announced a pretty brunette, who refused to reveal her name or age. "They must develop their bodies physically to gain self-confidence and to lessen their psychological dependence on men."

San Francisco *Chronicle,* January 14, 1970

Lt. Robert B. Johnson of the Berkeley Police Department will speak on "Defensive Tactics for Ladies" for members of the University of California Mothers Club on Tuesday.

Berkeley Gazette, February 25, 1971

Martial arts and self defense study offer a way of self reflection and change. As our concentration grows in our study, the focus involved is a clear meditative concentration permeating the wrenching pushing exertion of our bodies. We have here a way of experiencing the oneness of our mind/body/soul, healing in ourselves the fragmentations and divisions of patriarchy. The style I study is called Ja Shin Do, which in one translation means Art of the New Self.

Emily Erwin Culpepper, *Womanspirit,* Summer 1976

Women employees at the Long Island Jewish Medical Center are being taught forms of karate and ju-jitsu, since they are concerned about their personal safety when they have to walk to their cars in the parking lot at midnight and then drive through deserted streets to their homes.

Female Liberation Newsletter (Boston), August 2, 1971

After the workout/class, we spent the rest of our time talking about the meaning in our lives of martial art study. I shared information about some of the physiological aspects, that is—this kind of overall body workout often produces a calm, exhilarating feeling of well-being, which in part may be due to the stimulation of the right brain, which is so underused and undervalued in our patriarchal, linear, technical-mind culture. Also, for many women, our determination to study a martial art is often the first time we have really taken physical development and strength potential of our bodies seriously. For women with previous athletic backgrounds, martial art study often has a new sense of woman-identified purpose. I find that I learned the lessons of patriarchy in my muscles and sinews, as well as in my mind and soul; and this martial art study is both an UN-conditioning process, as well as the conditioning and creating of a new self.

Emily Erwin Culpepper, *Womanspirit,* Summer 1976

In Milan recently, 400 girls stormed a local high school. They punched teachers and staff, broke into a classroom and dragged out Sergio Brambilla, an 18-year-old student.

They shoved him into the school cafeteria, where they conducted their own trial. The girls accused Brambilla of raping his girlfriend in a car and then threatening her with a gun not to report him. The girls found him guilty and beat him severely.

Parade, June 26, 1977

Being in the Men's Auxiliary is a necessary but not a sufficient condition for making SCUM's escape list; it's not enough to do good; to save their worthless asses men must also avoid evil. A few examples of the most obnoxious or harmful types are: *rapists,* politicians and all who are in their service (campaigners, members of political parties, etc.); lousy singers and musicians; Chairmen of Boards; Breadwinners; landlords; owners of greasy spoons and restaurants that play Musak; "Great Artists"; cheap pikers; cops; tycoons; scientists working on death and destruction or for private industry (practically all scientists); liars and phonies; disc jockeys; men who intrude themselves in the slightest way on any strange female; real estate men; stock brokers; men who speak when they have nothing to say; men who loiter idly on the street and mar the landscape with their presence; double dealers; flim-flam artists; litterbugs, plagiarizers; men who in the slightest way harm any female [etc.].

Valerie Solanas, *SCUM Manifesto,* 1967

Battle Ground, Wash.: A man dressed as a delivery person entered the home of a 76-year-old woman Friday afternoon and attempted to force the woman to perform sexual acts, but was apparently rebuffed by the woman's stubbornness, the Clark County sheriff's office reported.

The woman was listed in satisfactory condition at Vancouver Memorial Hospital, being treated for bruises, minor stab wounds, and scrapes. . . .

[When] the man demanded she engage in sexual activities, the woman told her attacker, "I'm too old for that sort of thing," police said.

"She said she then turned down the hall and was going to the bathroom where she could lock herself in," a deputy reported.

Then the man picked up from a hallway table an inch-long knife the victim used for opening letters and threatened the victim with that, again demanding she engage in sexual acts, deputies said.

The woman told police she told the man, "That knife is too dull to cut anything."

The assailant knocked the woman to the floor and again attempted to coerce her into sexual acts. She bit him. The woman said the man took out a flashlight and hit her several times.

The man then left.

> *The Oregonian,* June 24, 1978

I've been working up in McKenzie. I've spent three months there, and boy, I'm sure hard up for a woman. Do you have time?

Shannon stared at him, while driving at 50 mph over the Granville Street bridge. It always made them uncomfortable.

Well, he said, I have an hour before the plane leaves and I sure am hard up for a woman.

There's hookers all over Davie and Granville, Shannon said at last. I'm a cab-driver.

Oh, I wasn't meaning you were a hooker. I wouldn't pay for it. Shit. . . .

A pig like you had better be prepared to pay, Shannon said, because you sure the hell will never get it for free.

Perverts are very sensitive. What did I do to you? he asked, hurt. Why are you insulting me?

You don't consider you insulted me?

No. Shit, no. I mean—You're a dame—And I'm not one of your ordinary construction workers, you know, I'm a *student*.
Helen Potrebenko, *Taxi*, 1975

Headline: *Armed Women Decoys in Campus Rapist Hunt* (Evanston, Ill.).
San Francisco *Chronicle*, June 9, 1973

Ann Arbor Women's Crisis Center puts out booklet, "Freedom from Rape," 1973

Los Angeles, February 1972 Anti-Rape Squad

Seattle, Anti-Rape Squad, 1972

Washington, D.C., Rape Crisis Center, 1973

North Virginia, Task Force on Rape, 1973

June 2, 1974. Two bills before Congress to establish a National Center for the Prevention and Control of Rape

Boston area members of Women Against Rape have established a 24-hour rape crisis center
The Spokeswoman, June 15, 1973

"Women, Rape and the Law"
A Community Service Program
Saturday, June 2, 1973
Palm Beach Junior College Gymnasium
Lake Worth, Fla.

The rape laws and the literature concerning them have been dominated by fears that false rape charges might result in the convictions of innocent men. The false complaint is feared more in rape cases than in other crimes because of the basic assumption that many women are either amoral or hostile to men and that women can induce rape convictions solely by virtue of fabricated reports.

The commentators, however, consistently have failed to document or closely analyze these assumptions. Nevertheless, these fears have produced and sustained laws and attitudes that seek to protect the innocent from an unjust rape conviction, rather than to protect women from rape.

Camille E. LeGrand, *California Law Review*, 1973, *61*

Madison, Wis.: When a 15-year-old boy raped a girl in a stairwell at West High School, Judge Archie Simonson ruled, he was reacting "normally" to prevalent sexual permissiveness and womens' provocative clothing.

The judge decreed that the youth—who was ruled a delinquent—should be permitted to stay at home under court supervision rather than placed in an institution or other rehabilitation center.

Yesterday about 40 women, one wearing a bikini, paraded outside Dane County Courthouse demanding the judge's resignation.

San Francisco *Chronicle*, May 27, 1977

[Judge Simonson] claimed nationwide support yesterday for his views on rape and told women to stop wearing provocative outfits and teasing men. . . .

"I'm trying to say to women, 'stop teasing,'" the judge added.

"There should be a restoration of modesty in dress and the elimination from the community of the sexual gratification businesses."

The 16-year-old victim was wearing tennis shoes, blue jeans and a blouse over a turtleneck sweater when she was attacked by three boys. Her screams for help were drowned out by the school band, rehearsing in a room near the stairwell.

San Francisco *Chronicle*, May 28, 1977

[Judge Simonson] said yesterday his views on sex may be old-fashioned but he vowed not to resign despite the recall move against him.

San Francisco *Chronicle*, July 30, 1977

The concept of victim precipitation hinges primarily on male definitions of expressed or implied consent to engage in sexual relations, and is shaped by traditional restrictive stereotypes of women. Thus, hitchhiking and walking alone at night in a rough neighborhood may be considered behavior encouraging a sexual attack. This view of what a *man* can assume to be a sexual invitation is unreasonable, but is so well engrained in society that women often accept it as well. As a result, a woman may react to being raped with considerable guilt and refuse to report the attack. A woman hitchhiker may later feel that she encouraged the rape simply by accepting a ride. Yet, when the female hitchhiker first sets out to get a ride, she normally is not expecting—or hoping for—a sexual encounter. A woman should not be made to feel guilty for acts that do not involve express sexual invitation, nor should she be denied the right to change her mind. In its failure to accord any consideration to the woman victim's intentions, victim precipitation becomes nothing more than a male view of the circumstances leading up to the incident.

Camille E. LeGrand, *California Law Review,* 1973, *61*

[Judge Simonson]: Even in open court we have people appearing—women appearing without bras and with the nipples fully exposed, and they think it is smart and they sit here on the witness stand with their dresses up over the cheeks of their butts, and we have this type of thing in the schools. . . .

Meryl Manhardt [prosecutor]: Your Honor, with all due respect, I find your remarks about women's clothing particularly sexist.

S.: You bet it is. I can't go around walking exposing my genitals like they can the mammary glands.

M.: You are reflecting the general theory that woman provokes an assault, and I cannot accept that idea.

S.: It sure raises a lot of interest in my mind from time to time.

San Francisco *Chronicle,* August, 26, 1977

Dane County voters decide today whether to remove Judge Archie Simonson from the bench for controversial remarks he made during a hearing on a juvenile rape case.

Simonson, 52, faces five opponents in a special election that could make him the first state official ousted from office since the recall amendment was adopted in 1926.

San Francisco *Chronicle,* September 7, 1977

"I wanted to be a lawyer because I believed if they chose to, they could make some differences," said Moria Krueger, the Dane County judge-elect, who had just won Wisconsin's first judicial recall election and will become the first woman elected judge in this capital city. . . .

She will take the seat of Archie Simonson [who was recalled Wednesday]. She also trounced four other candidates.

Simonson, 52, lost to Krueger by 8,809 votes out of 77,907 cast in the election.
San Francisco *Chronicle,* September 9, 1977

The fear of the maniac and the genuine desire to protect chaste, totally innocent women from sexual assault clash mightily with the fear of convicting innocent men. As a result, we have on one hand harsh penalties for rape; on the other, however, we have few convictions and a myriad of laws and attitudes that tend to protect men from conviction.
Camille E. LeGrand, *California Law Review,* 1973, *61*

Rape is a crime that is still very much with us; in fact, its growth rate is the highest of any violent crime—murder, robbery, and aggravated assault included.

The most recent FBI statistics reveal that reported rapes doubled from 27,620 in 1967 to an all-time high of 56,730 in 1976.
Sandy Hotchkiss, San Francisco *Chronicle,* December 3, 1978

One out of three women over the age of 14 will be raped sometime during her lifetime in Los Angeles County—according to statistics of the Los Angeles Ad Hoc Committee on Rape.

The RAPE CRISIS HOTLINE covers Los Angeles and the San Fernando Valley with 24-hour crisis counselling, information, support and referral. Counselors also accompany victims to the police, hospital and court upon request.
Sister, December 77/January 78

At first we were nameless, a group of friends responding to need: a woman who'd been threatened and assaulted by a former lover, was staying with a friend, but wanted to stay in her own home and was afraid to stay alone. We—7 or 8 of us—set up a schedule, 2 women a night for company and protection.

The results were cheerful but chaotic. This small group decided to set up a structure, a phone list, and a system to offer protection to women being threatened by abusive men. The plan was to stay with the women (mostly at night) in rotating groups of however many women the situation seemed to demand. . . .

Originally we were a confidential, closed group, partly because we were unsure of the legality of what we were doing; partly because we didn't want the abusive men we were protecting the women against to know who we were. This second level of confidentiality—our individual identities—still makes sense to us. About legal implications, we've discovered that when we go into a woman's home at her invitation, we are perfectly within the law.

> *The Godmothers: A Brief History* (pamphlet), Portland, Oregon, March 16, 1978

Rape Speak-Out, July 1972, San Francisco, downtown YWCA

Minneapolis Rape Counseling Center, 1973

Rape Crisis Center, Boston, publishes booklet: "Rape: Medical and Legal Information," 1973

Dade County, Florida, January 10, 1974, Jackson Memorial Hospital Rape Treatment Center opened

We've been talking around the office about some of the terms we use to describe the crimes which our work is against. *Wife abuse,* for example, is inaccurate and leaves out women abused by their sons, brothers, fathers, and boyfriends. *Battered woman* seems to some of us objectifying; think of calling a woman who's been raped a *raped woman,* as if the crime committed against her had somehow transformed her essence. Some of us feel the same way about using the term *victim* excessively, that the word assumes a split between us-on-call and them-calling. In fact many women working on the hotline have been victimized, and none of us would be here if we didn't feel strongly about our potential victimization. *Women victimized by family violence* seems the least offensive term, but it is cumbersome.

Incest is another problem term. Adult cousins or siblings choosing to relate sexually are clearly not the same as a grown man sexually abusing a girl child whose home he has access to, who may or may not be his kin. There should be a word that means "sexual abuse of a girl child by a male relative or pararelative."

There should also be one word that means "violence—sexual or not—against women." In a woman's language, there would be such a word (as the Eskimos have 14 or 18 words for snow).

Rape Relief Hotline Newsletter (Portland, Oregon), November 1977

It did flash through my mind, while I was in the cage. I remembered how I felt right after I was raped. I changed the way I dressed, where I went; I did everything I could not to be at all alluring or vulnerable in terms of my body as a woman, if I was in a public place where men would be present. So doing that performance in that cage was a cathartic thing for me. There I was doing, full out—being out there, full out, in front of men. And the safety in it was the fact that the cage was there. . . .

It was so marvelous to me, inside, it was like I was doing everything that I wasn't supposed to do, and I was doing it to the most extreme. It was like breaking all the rules of being a woman that the society sets up.

Interview with Arina Isaacson, performing artist, on her performance with other women in a monkey cage at the San Francisco Zoo, July 1978

we stand in a circle
we face out into the dark
we face danger
we're not afraid
we are so many
we reclaim the night

. . .

we make this vow
to ourselves and each other
to our daughters
we will extend this safe circle
until its boundaries dissolve
and its power is everywhere
and we are safe everywhere
all women safe everywhere

RITUAL: Portland Women's Night Watch 2nd Annual Flashlight March to Stop Violence Against Women and Children, August 25, 1978, in Melanie Kay, *We Speak in Code,* 1979

I often notice that the mirror reflects an image which makes me question myself, feel critical or dissatisfied with my appearance. I don't ignore it as trivial, because I recognize that the mirror is infested with a very common political poison, virus hollywoodius or televisioniensis, subtle pressure to measure up to a pattern designed to enslave. Just to free myself of that pressure isn't a magical operation. But hundreds of other women will use that mirror. So after I have cleared my own image of that false cloud, I usually perform some sort of magical activity to neutralize the poison. I pour suggestive energy into the mirror, encouraging anyone who might look in it to see herself in her true beauty. I reinforce the suggestion with all the power of my will and call on the Goddess of Beauty Herself, blessed Aphrodite, to banish that which would deny Her, as she exists in all of us.

Margi Gumpert, *Country Women,* April 1974

At least 20 films during the last two years served rape to their audiences. In almost none of those films has the rape been more than a plot point, a quick way of getting from here to there—of motivating a distraught husband or lover to kill rapists. Often, it has been less.

Aljean Hurmetz, San Francisco *Chronicle,* October 28, 1973

It is probably true that castration would stop the rapist being a rapist, and would stop the bugger from menacing small boys. It is wholly unlikely that the operation would turn such people into well-adjusted members of society.

New Statesman, October 27, 1967

Two very successful revues have been staged by a group of women who have formed the Westbeth Playwrights Collective in Manhattan. Rape-In, their first show, began as a workshop project last year and was suggested by a man in the then mixed group. But it was the women who completed the assignment. When they did, they discovered they were all feminists.

Rape-In was divided into halves—women as victims and women as aggressors. A scene by Dolores Walker portrayed the offstage rape of a construction worker by a band of harpies. "Our consciousness was raised by the show," Dolores reports. "We saw that in the second half, some of the women acted not only aggressively but neg-

atively. What we were doing was copying the male power structure.
So we decided that in the next show—Up!—we would evolve it further."

Ms., August 1972

> I look down at the city
> which meant life to me, not death
> and think that somewhere there
> a cold center, composed
> of pieces of human beings
> metabolized, restructured
> by a process they do not feel
> is spreading in our midst
> and taking over our minds
> a thing that feels neither
> guilt nor rage: that is unable
> to hate, therefore to love.

Adrienne Rich, from "Merced," *Diving into the Wreck,* 1973

Humanity has never shown any regret for this horror [witchburn-
ing] in its cultural works . . . and no calling for an accounting has
occurred for us as it did for the Jews at Nuremburg. All women are
still seen as witches, and the fear of us has made it nearly impossible
to ascend into a love of our own sex.

Z. Budapest, *Plexus,* November 1978

Death and disfiguration.

One Christmas eve my lovers and I
we left the bar, driving home slow
there was a woman lying in the snow
by the side of the road. She was wearing
a bathrobe and no shoes, where were
her shoes? she had turned the snow
pink, under her feet. She was an Asian
woman, didn't speak much English, but
she said a taxi driver beat her up
and raped her, throwing her out of his
car
what on earth was she doing there
on a street she helped to pay for

but doesn't own?
doesn't she know to stay home?

I am a pervert, therefore I've learned
to keep my hands to myself in public
but I was so drunk that night,
I actually did something loving
I took her in my arms, this woman,
until she could breathe right, and
my friends who are perverts too
they touched her too
we all touched her.
"You're going to be all right"
we lied. She started to cry
"I'm 55 years old" she said
and that said everything.

Six big policemen answered the call
no child *in* them.
they seemed afraid to touch her.
then grabbed her like a corpse and heaved her
on their metal stretcher into the van,
crashing and clumsy.
She was more frightened than before.
they were cold and bored.
'don't leave me' she said.
'she'll be all right' they said.
    Judy Grahn, from *A Woman is Talking to Death,* 1974

But how hard it is, when we are struggling with fears, to think beyond ourselves and the present moment. Even the most responsible of us is not in a learning mood on those days, days which sometimes stretch into years, years when the quiet voice of reason is drowned out by the cries of the terrorized child within us. Time is meaningless then. How can we master it enough to swing our intelligence up and down the decades, the centuries, scanning them to see what marks our acts are leaving on them?
    Lillian Smith, *The Journey,* 1965

This is a tape about rape we're making. It began because Nellie and I were once talking as we were waiting for the elevator. We were saying how we were so scared just to live alone, and we just had tremendous fear of anything happening at night and in the apartment. We discovered that the reason we were both scared was because we had both been raped and that being raped had long-lasting effects on us.

> Noreen Connell and Cassandra Wilson (Eds.), *Rape: The First Sourcebook for Women* 1974

A five-year follow-up study of rape victims, completed by Dr. Ann Burgess of Boston College and Lynda L. Homstrom, indicates that rape recovery periods vary according to the type of attack a woman experiences. Recovery periods researched in the study lasted from a few months to over five years. Data shows that victims of a random attack take much longer to recover than those who can make some rational explanation for what happened to them.

Those who have the worst time recovering are women who are attacked in their own beds and women deprived of social and emotional support.

One unexpected finding in the study reveals that victims who coped successfully in the past with the loss of a parent or child recovered faster than those without such a history.

The overwhelming majority of the women were profoundly affected by their rape. Forty-two percent rated it as the most upsetting event of their lives.

> *The Longest Revolution,* June 1978

Mind is the soul, mind against fear is a faith dealer and does not smell the alarming animal.

> Georgette Cerutti, "That Bone Place Where There Is Light," *Conditions,* II, 1977

Having witch craft, the craft of witches, is having power over your own life. That is why it is and always has been dangerous to the state, the system.

> Alice Molloy, *In Other Words,* 1977

We take as our source the hitherto unrecognized culture of women, a culture which from long experience of oppression developed an intense appreciation for life, a sensitivity to unspoken thoughts and the complexity of simple things, a powerful knowledge of human needs and feelings.

> Redstockings of the Women's Liberation Movement, "Principles," 1971

To re-source is to find another source, an entirely different and prior one, a source deeper than the partriarchy and one that allows us to stand in the path of continuous and cosmic energy.
Sally Gearhart "Through the Looking Glass," keynote address, Women's Spirituality Conference, April 1976, Boston, in *Womanspirit,* Summer 1976

This new spiritual inquiry has challenged and further broken down patriarchal authority—the authority of patriarchal science and religion. At the same time, this broadening of our vision of reality cannot help but have a formative and creative impact on the development of our female culture—as inspiration and material for our art, music, literature, esthetics, *and* by adding a profound new dimension to our relations with one another.
Susan Rennie and Kirsten Grimstad, *Quest,* Spring 1975

That women in the United States and elsewhere have begun to claim sacred space for themselves, to create rituals which emphasize their loyalty to each other and finally name the powers which men have found "anomalous" (i.e., nameless) is indeed an ultimate, radical (proceeding from the root) affirmation of the revolutionary potential of the feminist movement. Asserting the right to ritual means as a source of power, vision and solidarity is the symbolic corollary of equal pay, choice of abortion, domestic freedom, the establishment of women's businesses, etc. Successful and enduring change in the status of women will come only through the parallel transformation of symbols and realities. Feminist ritual practice is currently the most important model for symbolic and, therefore, psychic and spiritual change in women.
Kay Turner, *Heresies,* Spring 1978

Two trucks driving on the road. Is this real? Ignore it, it will go away. Headlights piercing the soft moonlight, engines roaring, drunken men's shouts. Women's heads turn. . . . Fear ripples through the crowd. . . . "A cone of white light." Women surrounded the circle, the campsites, with white light. Women chanted low and quiet, gradually building in energy. Women stayed in the circle. The drummers kept drumming. "Don't give them any energy." Women softly chanting. "Go away. Go away." Women visualizing the truck keeping going, not stopping, going out. A giant hand pushing the truck down the road. . . . And the truck drove on past us and out, never stopping. The other truck finally got started and roared away. One of the men fell out, ran after the truck shouting, "Don't leave me! Don't leave me!"

Hallie Iglehart, *Womanspirit*, Fall 1975

Most women interested or involved in feminist concepts of spirituality do not regard this spirituality as an end in itself but as a means of gaining and giving strength and understanding that will help us to confront the many tangible and material issues of the blatant inequalities of society as we know it today.

Merlin Stone, *Heresies*, Spring 1978

My name is Wanda Carr. I am 40 years old. My husband beat and abused me for years. I shot him. I was acquitted. California.

ALL: I AM A WOMAN. I FOUGHT BACK.

My name is Marlene Roan Eagle. I am an Oglala Sioux and I am 20 years old. My husband beat me several times. Twice I was hospitalized from these beatings, once for a month. When I was 7 months pregnant, he beat me with a broom handle. I grabbed a knife and stabbed him. I was found not guilty, on grounds of defense of my unborn child. Ohio.

ALL: I AM A WOMAN. I FOUGHT BACK.

My name is Inez Garcia. I killed the man who held me down while his friends raped me. I spent 19 months in prison, my case was 3 years in the courts. I was found not guilty. California.

ALL: I AM A WOMAN. I FOUGHT BACK.

My name is Gloria Maldonado. I am 32 years old. When my husband attacked me and our son, I shot him. I was not prosecuted, on grounds of "insufficient evidence." Chicago, Illinois.

ALL: I AM A WOMAN. I FOUGHT BACK.

My name is Virginia Tierce. I shot the man who raped me. I was found guilty of manslaughter. I was granted a retrial. I was acquitted.

ALL: I AM A WOMAN. I FOUGHT BACK.

RITUAL: Portland Women's Night Watch 2nd Annual Flashlight March to Stop Violence Against Women and Children, August 25, 1978. Parts were read by eight women in masks.

And I've learned once again that the stronger we become, the more demands are made on us. The more healing we learn, the more seriously in need are the people who come to us. The more visibly powerful and loving we become, the more threatening we are to a society that functions by keeping people, and especially women, powerless and alienated from one another.

Hallie Iglehart, *Womanspirit,* Fall 1975

Some feminists see themselves as exclusively "political feminists" or as "spiritual feminists," and many find it difficult to understand the other's point of view. The spiritualists feel that the politicalists are too narrow or insensitive to what they regard as "a more encompassing feminist consciousness," whereas the politicalists consider the spiritualists impractical and believe that they avoid "the reality of the real political issues." I think that it is extremely important for us to realize that this division between the spiritual and the political is arbitrary and unnecessarily divisive.

Judith Todd, *Heresies,* Spring 1978

In putting together this issue on the Great Goddess, Women's Spirituality, we wanted to offer a holistic concept of the Goddess and to move beyond an inside/outside duality. We also recognized a need to counter the distrust that most women harbor towards religion and any aspect of spirituality because of the oppression that we have all experienced from patriarchal religions.

Editorial Statement, *Heresies,* Spring 1978

It is the object and center of the whole Law to abolish idolatry and utterly uproot it, and to overthrow the opinion that any of the stars could interfere for good or evil in human matters, because it leads to the worship of stars. It was therefore necessary to slay all witches as being undoubtedly idolators. . . . But in all performances of witchcraft it is laid down as a rule that women should be employed in the chief operation; and therefore the Law says, "Thou shalt not suffer a witch to live."

Maimonides, *The Guide for the Perplexed,* 1956

The first phase of the current battle/war passes: the breaking of the symbolic power of the phallos in crucial areas . . . the overall consciousness of the civilization, at least in this country, is definitely

for the first time, in our lifetime, questioning that power, if only by virtue of being aware that that is where the center of power is, in this civilization. . . . We have broken that power symbolically in crucial areas.
          Alice Molloy, *In Other Words,* 1977

As Western religions entered a state of alienation from the body, nature and this world, women were denigrated because they seemed more carnal, fleshy, and earthy than the culture creating males. . . . The denigration of the female body and its powers is further expressed in Western culture's attitudes toward childbirth. . . . The women's liberation movement aided the advocates of natural childbirth and home birth by emphasizing the need for women to control and take pride in their bodies.
    The symbol of the Goddess aids this process of naming and reclaiming the female body and its functions. In the ancient world and among modern women, the Goddess symbol represents the birth, death, and rebirth processes of the natural and human worlds. The female body is viewed as a direct expression or incarnation, of waxing and waning, life and death cycles in the universe.
          Carol P. Christ, *Heresies,* Spring 1978

Historian Vincent Scully maintains that not even the palaces were of greatest architectural importance on Crete. He believes that their siting in the landscape was more important. Typically each temple, here as well as throughout Greece, was built in an enclosed valley and aligned on a north/south axis to have a view across the valley of a conical hill, and beyond that, to a horned or double-peaked mountain that contained a cave sanctuary. At the Palace of Knossos, these features were sited/sighted through the Horns of Consecration. The proper siting of the palace accentuated the meaning of the landscape as the body of the Goddess. The valley was her encircling arms; the conical hill, her breast or nurturing function; the horned mountains, her "lap" or cleft vulva, the Earth's active power; and the cave sanctuary, her birth-giving womb.
          Mimi Lobell, *Heresies,* Spring 1978

For as regards intellect, or the understanding of spiritual things, they seem to be of a different nature from men.
          Heinrich Kramer and James Sprenger, *Malleus Maleficarum,* 1971 (orig. pub. 1486)

Long before the influential oracular site of Delphi was seized by Apollo, it was a sacred part of the body of the Earth Mother Gaea. From a seismic cleft in this "body of Gaea," exuded intoxicating gases that induced prophetic visions. Apollo killed the great Python, protector of the site; thereafter Pythia, the priestess who pronounced the prophecies, spoke for Apollo rather than Gaea.

Mimi Lobell, *Heresies,* Spring 1978

We found wherever there are feminist communities, women are exploring psychic and nonmaterial phenomena; reinterpreting astrology; creating and celebrating feminist rituals around birth, death, menstruation; reading the Tarot; studying prepatriarchal forms of religion; reviving and exploring esoteric goddess-centered philosophies such as Wicce; developing and cultivating dream analysis, ESP, astral projection, precognition; learning psychic and homeopathic healing; rescuing the holistic perspective of the right hemisphere of the brain from the contempt of the left-brained linear-mindedness; practicing meditation and yoga; rewriting the *I Ching;* revolutionizing our food and natural resource consciousness of our connectedness with the rest of the biosphere.

Susan Rennie and Kirsten Grimstad, *Quest,* Spring 1975

Thus the witches sometimes order: take a leaf of a certain plant, when the moon is seen in a certain degree . . . also a certain quantity of the horn, the sweat, the hair, and blood of a certain animal when the sun is, e.g., in the middle of the sky . . . and a portion of a certain mineral . . . melted at a certain conjunction of sun and moon, and a definite position of the stars; speak then, and say certain words, and fumigate with those leaves . . . to that molten image, and such and such a thing will happen. . . . In most cases the condition is added that women must perform these actions. Thus it is stated in reference to the means of obtaining rain that ten virgins dressed with diadems and red garments should dance.

Maimonides, *The Guide for the Perplexed,* 1956

It has emerged from feminist consciousness, an inkling or more of the first aspect and perhaps ever-present search for answers to such theological questions as the possible purposes (or nonpurpose) of existence, the true nature of morality (or immorality), birth, death, and the nature of the mind as it is revealed in intelligence, intuition, and reason. For many centuries, women have been taught that if they cared to consider these questions at all (the implication being that such questions were actually too abstract for female minds) answers were to be found in the words and writings of male priests, male ministers, male rabbis and male gurus.

Merlin Stone, *Heresies,* Spring 1978

On the most immediate level, in my work, I am trying to write poems that are free of the institutionalized conflicts and brutality that have characterized our literary tradition for so long, to use simple grammar and syntax, and to praise, praise.

Olga Broumas, *Heresies,* Fall 1977

I told of my experiences with the grove of trees from which Ruth and I have taken our names. The place was a meditation/intuition source for us for three years until we were forced to leave the commune because of our feminist politics. We had developed simple silent rituals and agreed not to change anything in the grove. Without realizing it, in these ways we were creating a space for intuition to come to us. I began to embrace trees and listen for guidance, but then condemned myself for this freaky behavior. Ruth supported my continuing it and encouraged me to write down what I "heard" there. These records in my journals have been very helpful.

Jean Mountaingrove, *Womanspirit,* Summer 1976

In authentic ritual experience, something, an ability to break through the present, is available which can lead to discovery and creativity. Ritual is a potent source of invention because the participants feel the extreme intensity, sometimes the ecstasy, of openness to possibility and revelation. This sense of extreme openness and creativity is rare for women who have been traditionally circumscribed by severe limitation, constrained by custom, with no hope for a changed future.

Kay Turner, *Heresies,* Spring 1978

Some say they find this force within themselves; others regard it as external. Some feel it in the ocean, the moon, a tree, the flight of a bird or in the constant stream of coincidences (or noncoincidences) that occur in our lives. Some find access to it in the lighting of a candle, chanting, meditating alone or with other women . . .

Merlin Stone, *Heresies,* Spring 1978

Spirituality is so threatening because it is absolutely predicated upon self-trust.

> Juanita Weaver, *Womanspirit,* Fall 1975

She looked up over her knitting and met the third stroke and it seemed to her like her own eyes meeting her own eyes, searching as she alone could search into her mind and her heart, purifying out of existence that lie, any lie. She praised herself in praising the light, without vanity, for she was stern, she was searching, she was beautiful like that light. It was odd, she thought, how if one was alone, one leant to inanimate things; trees, streams, flowers; felt they expressed one; felt they became one; felt they knew one, in a sense were one; felt an irrational tenderness thus (she looked at that long steady light) as for oneself.

> Virginia Woolf, *To the Lighthouse,* 1927

Connections are made slowly, sometimes they grow underground.
You cannot tell always by looking what is happening.
More than half a tree is spread out in the soil under your feet.

> Marge Piercy, from "The Influence Coming into Play: The Seven of Pentacles," *To Be of Use,* 1973

Now, think over what I'm saying. There may be a way to help us get back. The medicine is dangerous, in which lies its power. Stand before a mirror. Just keep eye contact until you've said hello. Rest on the stream of feeling flowing through your eyes. Know the safety of that place where you ARE all change. Cry in your face—hurting sorrow. Cross your hands and begin to touch—life starts to flow. Masturbate to water roses, feel the color come. Cross your eyes a new dimension. Vision of the Eye. Twinkling lights dance over the surface. Through the mirror to the other side. The Goddess is you, in your image.

The gift of the Goddess is body to soul, soul to body. Imagine the energy if we all looked at once. The Patriarchy could not stand such a blow. They took our bodies away by forbidding the looking. They said we were objects and they had the eyes. But they can never kill Her, only try to get us to knock ourselves off. And we'll never do it. Her reflections are scattered through their dark halls.

Remember the past. The Goddess grows restless. All alone I can't stand the heat of Her energy. Help me, sisters. Look in the mirror.

> Martha Alsup, *Heresies,* Spring 1978

As women we are coming to know the power of consciousness—it is energy that participates in the coalescence of the events that happen to us. From the beginning of each of our lives, we've been systematically trained to experience ourselves as vulnerable, as weak sexual objects. No longer can we allow ourselves to feel like victims only to attract those looking for a likely object. We must dig deep into the roots of our experience, extract all these feelings and throw them into the face of the patriarchy; replacing them with our strength and power, thereby entering a new dimension of life—leaving all rapists behind with no victims to be found.

Margo Adair, teacher of applied meditation

Appendix
Rape Crisis Centers

This list was compiled from the 1981 edition of *National Directory: Rape Prevention and Treatment Resources,* published by the National Center for the Prevention and Control of Rape and for sale by the Superintendent of Documents, U.S. Government Printing Office, Washington, D.C. 20402.

If you would like additional information on rape or sexual assault, please contact the following:

National Center for the Prevention and Control of Rape
National Institute of Mental Health
Room 15-99, Parklawn Building
5600 Fishers Lane
Rockville, MD 20857
(301) 443-1910
(interdisciplinary perspective)

National Center on Child Abuse and Neglect
P.O. Box 1182
Washington, DC 20013
(202) 755-8208
(child sexual assault)

National Criminal Justice Reference Service
P.O. Box 6000
Rockville, MD 20850
(202) 862-2900
(criminal justice perspective)

National Library of Medicine
National Institute of Health
Building 38
8600 Rockville Pike
Bethesda, MD 20014
(301) 496-5116
(bibliographic searches of professional literature)

Alabama

South Central Alabama Mental Health
Center/Helpline
P.O. Box 1028, Andalusia 36024
(800) 932-0501

Rape Response Program
3600 8th Ave S, Birmingham 35222
(205) 323-7273

Wiregrass Comprehensive Mental
Health Center
Rape Prevention and Control Services
104 Prevatt Rd, P.O. Drawer 1245
Dothan 36302
(205) 794-0300 *(hotline);*
(205) 794-0731

C.E.D. Mental Health Center
901 Goodyear Ave, Gadsden 35901
(205) 492-7800

Council Against Rape/Lighthouse
830 S Court St, P.O. Box 4622
Montgomery 36104
(205) 263-4481

Indian Rivers Community Mental
Health Center
1915 6th St, Tuscaloosa 35403
(205) 345-1600

Russell University Health Service
Mental Health Section
P.O. Box Y, University 35486
(205) 348-6262

Alaska

Standing Together Against Rape
430 W 7th Ave, Suite 205
Anchorage 99510
(907) 276-7273 *(hotline);*
(907) 277-0222 *(week nights, weekends)*

Tundra Women's Coalition
P.O. Box 1034, Bethel 99559
(907) 543-3455 or 3456

Women in Crisis—Counseling and
Assistance, Inc. (WICCA)
331 Fifth Ave, Fairbanks 99701
(907) 452-7273 *(hotline);*
(907) 452-2293 *(office)*

Women in Safe Homes
P.O. Box 6552, Ketchikan 99901
(907) 225-2730

Bering Sea Women's Group
P.O. Box 1596, Nome 99762
(907) 443-5444

Women's Resource Center
Rape Intervention Program
P.O. Box 2464, Spur Rd
Soldotna 99669
(907) 262-5273

Arizona

Coconino Community Guidance Center,
Inc.
519 N Leroux, Flagstaff 86001
(602) 774-3351

City of Glendale
Victim Assistance Services
7012 N 58th Dr, Glendale 85302
(602) 931-5593

Arizona Women's Commission
1700 W Washington, Rm 810 West
Wing, Phoenix 85007
(602) 255-3609

Center Against Sexual Assault (CASA)
1131 E Missouri, Phoenix 85014
(602) 257-8095 (*hotline*);
(602) 279-9824 (*office*)

National Organization for Women—
Phoenix Chapter
P.O. Box 16023, Phoenix 85011
(602) 252-3955

Crisis Intervention Unit
Scottsdale Police Department
3739 Civic Center, Scottsdale 85251
(602) 994-2593

Pima County Attorney's Victim
Witness Program
111 W Congress St, Suite 900
Tucson 85701
(602) 792-8021

Pima County Health Department
8230 E Broadway, Suite E-10
Tucson 85711
(602) 885-6705

Tucson Rape Crisis Center, Inc.
P.O. Box 843, Tucson 87502
(602) 623-7273 (*hotline*);
(602) 624-7273 (*office*)

Tucson Women's Commission
1515 E Broadway, Tucson 85719

Arkansas

Rape Crisis Service
P.O. Box 2887, Station A
3111 S 70th St, Fort Smith 72913
(501) 452-6650

Ovachita Regional Counseling and
Mental Health Center
P.O. Box 1106, 124 Rugg St
Hot Springs 71901
(501) 624-7111

Rape Crisis, Inc.
P.O. Box 5181, Hillcrest Station
Little Rock 72205
(501) 375-5181

California

Rape Crisis Network Unit
503 N Anaheim Blvd, Anaheim 92805
(714) 776-3004

Sexual Behavior Laboratory
Atascadero State Hospital
Drawer A, Atascadero 93422
(805) 466-2200

Sexual Orientation Program
10333 El Camino Real
Atascadero 93422
(805) 466-2200, ext 78 or 79

Auburn Women's Center
Placer Rape Crisisline
701 High St, Rm 201, Auburn 95603
(916) 885-5571 (*Auburn hotline*);
(916) 624-5571 (*Roseville hotline*);
(916) 885-0443 (*office*)

Child Sexual Abuse Treatment
Program
Special Problems Unit
Kern County Mental Health Services
Department
1960 Flower St, Bakersfield 93305
(805) 861-2251

Henrietta Weill Child Guidance Clinic
804 11th St, Bakersfield 93304
(805) 327-7914

Bay Area Women Against Rape
P.O. Box 240, Berkeley 94703
(415) 845-7273

Berkeley Women's Center
2955 Telegraph Ave, Berkeley 94705
(415) 548-4343; (415) 548-7829

Rape Prevention Education Program
University of California
363 Cowell Hospital, Berkeley 94720
(415) 642-7202

Women's History Research Center, Inc.
2325 Oak St, Berkeley 94708
(415) 548-1770

Rape Crisis Intervention of North
Central California
P.O. Box 423, Chico 95927
(916) 342-7273

Project Sister Rape Crisis Service
520 N Indian Hill Blvd
Claremont 91711
(714) 626-4357

Rape Prevention Steering Committee
c/o Shari Speer, Toll Hall
Scripps College, Claremont 91711
(714) 621-8000, ext 2272

Child Sexual Abuse Treatment
Program of Contra Costa County
1600 Galindo St, Concord 94520
(415) 798-4575

Rape Crisis Service of Concord
1950 Parkside Dr, Concord 94520
(415) 798-7273

Yolo County Sexual Assault Center
203 F St, Davis 95616
(916) 758-8400 (*Davis hotline*);
(916) 662-1133 (*Woodland hotline*);
(916) 371-1907 (*E Yolo hotline*);
(916) 758-0540 (*office*)

Rape Emergency Assistance League
of San Diego County (R.E.A.L.)
P.O. Box 468, El Cajon 92020
(714) 466-7273 (*hotline*);
(714) 464-4457 (*office*)

El Cerrito Police Department
10900 San Pablo Ave, El Cerrito 94530
(415) 237-2123

Child Sexual Abuse Treatment
Program of Humboldt County
929 Koster, Eureka 95501
(707) 445-7711

Child Sexual Abuse Treatment
Program
Solano County Mental Health
Department
1408 Pennsylvania Ave, Fairfield 94533
(707) 429-6521

Upper Solano County Rape Crisis
Service
P.O. Box 368, Fairfield 94533
(707) 422-7273

Community Assistance in Assault and
Rape Emergency (CAARE Project,
Inc.)
650 N Main St, Fort Bragg 95437
(707) 964-4357

Victim Assistance for the Sexually
Traumatized (VAST Project)
38218 Glenmoor Dr, Suite A
Fremont 94536
(415) 792-7000

Victim Services Project
Fremont Police Department
39710 Civic Center Dr, Fremont 94538
(415) 791-4444

Child Abuse Program
School of Education
California State University
Fresno 93740
(209) 487-2912

Child Sexual Abuse Treatment
Program
Fresno County Department of Social
Services Family Crisis Center
1044 Fulton Mall, Suite 519
Fresno 93721
(209) 268-5391

Rape Counseling Service of Fresno,
Inc.
1660 M St, Fresno 93721
(209) 222-7273 (*hotline*);
(209) 486-4692 (*office*)

Victim/Witness Service Center
P.O. Box 453, Fresno 93709
(209) 488-3425

Santa Barbara Rape Crisis Center
5679 Hollister Ave, Goleta 93017
(805) 963-1696 (*hotline*);
(805) 964-5887 (*office*)

Southern Alameda County Women
Against Rape (SACWAR)
P.O. Box 662, Hayward 94541
(415) 582-7273

Irvine Community Against Rape
Everywhere (I.C.A.R.E.)
P.O. Box 4031, Irvine 92717
(714) 830-6111

Laguna Beach Free Clinic Rape Crisis
Unit
460 Ocean Ave, Laguna Beach 92651
(714) 494-0761

Hope Community Mental Health
Center and Pacoima Memorial Hospital
11600 Eldridge Ave
Lake View Terrace 91342
(213) 896-1161

Lompoc Rape Crisis Center
P.O. Box 148, Lompoc 93436
(805) 736-8913

Long Beach Rape Hotline
P.O. Box 14377, Long Beach 90803
(213) 597-2002

YWCA Emergency House
3636 Atlantic Ave, Long Beach 90807
(213) 595-1271 (day number only);
(213) 432-5471

California State University
at Los Angeles
Department of Physical Education and
Athletics
5151 State University Dr
Los Angeles 90032
(213) 224-3216

Center for the Pacific-Asian Family
Pacific-Asian Rape Care-Line
1514 W Olympic Blvd, Rm 323
Los Angeles 90015
(213) 388-0446

Crime Prevention Unit
Attorney General's Office
California Department of Justice
3580 Wilshire Blvd, 9th Floor
Los Angeles 90010
(213) 736-2366

East Los Angeles Rape Crisis Center,
Inc.
P.O. Box 63245, Los Angeles 90063
(213) 262-0944 (bilingual hotline);
(213) 267-2824 (office)

Kedren Community Mental Health
Center
Consultation and Education
Department
710 E 111th Place, Los Angeles 90059
(213) 777-1411

Los Angeles Commission on Assaults
Against Women
5410 Wilshire Blvd, No. 311
Los Angeles 90036
(213) 392-8381

Rape Response Service
Thalians Community Mental Health
Center
Cedar-Sinai Medical Center
8730 Alden Dr, Los Angeles 90048
(213) 855-3506 (hotline);
(213) 855-3530 (office)

Sexual Offenders Program
Institute of Law and Psychiatry
University of Southern California
1935 N Hospital Place, Graduate Hall
Rm 235
Los Angeles 90033
(213) 226-4942

Victim Witness Advocate Program
210 W Temple St, Rm 12-311
Los Angeles 90012
(213) 974-3531

People Against Rape
P.O. Box 2068, Merced 95340
(209) 383-2818

Rape Crisis Center of the Monterey
Peninsula
P.O. Box 862, Monterey 93940
(408) 375-4357

Child Sexual Abuse Treatment
Program of Napa County
Napa County Mental Health Services
2344 Old Sonoma Rd, Napa 94558
(707) 253-4561

San Fernando Valley Child Guidance
Clinic
9650 Zelzah Ave, Northridge 91325
(213) 993-9311

Parental Stress Service
5297 College Ave, Oakland 94618
(415) 655-8988

Victim/Witness Assistance Bureau
Alameda County District Attorney's
Office
Oakland Superior Court
1225 Fallon, Oakland 94612
(415) 874-7618

Orange County Rape Crisis Hotline
P.O. Box 2572, Orange 92669
(714) 831-9110

Mid-Peninsula Rape Crisis Center
4161 Alma St, Palo Alto 94306
(415) 493-7273 (*hotline*);
(415) 494-0972 (*office*)

Women Against Sexual Abuse
(WASA)
P.O. Box 937, Paramount 90723
(213) 868-3783

Huntington Memorial Hospital
Emergency Room
100 Congress St, Pasadena 91103
(213) 440-5111

Rape Emergency Assistance Crisis
Telephone (REACT)
Pasadena–Foothill Valley YWCA
78 N Marengo Ave, Pasadena 91101
(213) 973-3385 (*hotline*);
(213) 973-5171 (*office*)

East County Rape Crisis Unit
P.O. Box 1396, Pittsburg 94565
(415) 439-7273

H.E.R.E. Rape Crisis Clinic (Help
Eliminate Rape Everywhere)
516 N Placentia Ave, Placentia 92670
(714) 524-5040 (*hotline*);
(714) 528-6642 (*office*)

Parents United of Orange County
P.O. Box 1024, Placentia 92670
(714) 834-2583

Riverside Area Rape Crisis Center
3775 14th St, Riverside 92501
(714) 686-7273

Sacramento County District Attorney
Victim/Witness Program
901 G St, Sacramento 95814
(916) 443-2637, 443-2730 or 444-0520,
ext 386

Sacramento Rape Crisis Center
2104 Capitol Ave, Sacramento 95816
(916) 447-7273 (*hotline*);
(916) 447-3223 (*office*)

Child Sexual Abuse Treatment
Program
139 E Court St, San Bernardino 92410
(714) 885-6843

San Bernardino Rape Crisis
Intervention Services
1875 N "D" St, San Bernardino 92405
(714) 882-5291 (*hotline*);
(714) 883-8689 (*office*)

San Clemente Crisis Intervention
Center
P.O. Box 3687, San Clemente 92672
(714) 492-3264

Committee on Sexual Assault and
Intra-Family Violence
City Advisory Board on Women
202 C St, San Diego 92101
(714) 436-7137

San Diego County Child Sexual Abuse
Treatment Program
6950 Levant St, San Diego 92111
(714) 560-3082

Sex Crimes Detail and Homicide
San Diego Police Department
801 W Market St, San Diego 92101
(714) 236-6598

Child and Adolescent Sexual Abuse
Resource Center
San Francisco General Hospital
Bldg 80, Ward 83, Rm 318
1001 Potrero, San Francisco 94110
(415) 821-8386

Crime Prevention Unit
350 McAllister St, Rm 1096
San Francisco 94102
(415) 557-1150

Defense Against Rape Program
City College of San Francisco
Ocean and Phelan
San Francisco 94112
(415) 239-3420; (415) 564-5951

Delancey Street Foundation, Inc.
2563 Divisadero, San Francisco 94115
(415) 563-5326

San Francisco Women Against Rape
3543 18th St, San Francisco 94110
(415) 647-7273; 861-2024

Sexual Trauma Services
50 Ivy St, San Francisco 94121
(415) 558-3824

University of California Rape
Treatment Center
401 Parnassus Ave
San Francisco 94143
(415) 681-8080, ext 394

Rape Prevention and Education
Committee
San Jose State University
Counseling Services, Adm 201
San Jose 95192
(408) 277-2262

Santa Clara County Chapter of Parents
United/Daughters and Sons United
P.O. Box 952, San Jose 95108
(408) 292-8342

Sexual Abuse Treatment Program
Santa Clara County Juvenile Probation
Department
840 Guadalupe Pkwy, San Jose 95110
(408) 299-2475

Theorem Institute
1782 Technology Dr, San Jose 95110
(408) 294-1427; (800) 538-6896

YWCA—Valley Rape Crisis Center
375 S 3rd St, San Jose 95112
(408) 287-3000 (*hotline*);
(408) 295-4011 (*office*)

Victim/Witness Assistance Program
District Attorney's Office
Courthouse Annex
San Luis Obispo 93401
(805) 549-5800

Women's Resource Center
4070 Mission Ave, San Luis Rey 92068
(714) 757-3500

Children's Services
Social Services Division
San Mateo County Department of
Public Health and Welfare
225 37th Ave, San Mateo 94403
(415) 573-2765

San Mateo Women Against Rape
P.O. Box 6299, San Mateo 94401
(415) 349-7273

Rape Crisis Center of West Contra
Costa
c/o Brookside Hospital
Vale Rd, San Pablo 94806
(415) 236-7273

Marin County Child Sexual Abuse
Treatment Program
Child Protective Services Unit
Department of Social Services
P.O. Box 4160, Civic Center Branch
San Rafael 94903
(415) 479-0383

Marin Rape Crisis Center
P.O. Box 392, San Rafael 94902
(415) 924-2100

Child Sexual Abuse Treatment Team
1623 W 17th St, Santa Ana 92702
(714) 834-2583

CALM: Child Abuse Listening
Mediation, Inc.
P.O. Box 718, Santa Barbara 93102
(805) 966-9762

Santa Cruz Women Against Rape
P.O. Box 711, Santa Cruz 95061
(408) 426-7273

Women's Crisis Support
640 Capitola Rd, Santa Cruz 95062
(408) 425-2058 (*hotline*);
(408) 688-4551 (*shelter for battered
women*)

Santa Maria Valley Rape Crisis Center
224A N Benwiley, Santa Maria 93454
(805) 922-7273 (*hotline*);
(805) 922-8592 (*office*)

Rape Treatment Center
Santa Monica Hospital Medical Center
1225 15th St, Santa Monica 90404
(213) 451-1511

Rape Crisis Center of Sonoma County
P.O. Box 1426, Santa Rosa 95402
(707) 545-7273 (*hotline*);
(707) 545-7270 (*office*)

Rape Crisis Center of San Joaquin
County
P.O. Box 4803, Stockton 95204
(209) 465-4997 (*hotline*);
(209) 465-8969 (*office*)

Los Angeles Commission on Assaults
Against Women
Los Angeles Rape and Battering
Hotline
P.O. Box 145, Venice 90291
(213) 392-8381 (*hotline*);
(213) 938-3661 (*office*)

Women's Perspectives
P.O. Box 66, Visalia 93277
(209) 686-8651

Colorado

Sexual Assault Task Force
Aspen Mental Health Clinic
P.O. Box 2330, Aspen 81611
(303) 925-5400

Victim/Witness Assistance Program
District Attorney's Office
P.O. Box 471, Boulder 80303
(303) 441-3730

Buena Vista Correctional Facility
Box R, Buena Vista 81211
(303) 395-2418, ext 257

Rape Crisis Service
12 N Meade St,
Colorado Springs 80909
(303) 471-4357 (*hotline*);
(303) 633-4601 (*office*)

Victim Service Division
119 N Nevada Ave
Colorado Springs 80903
(303) 471-6616

Dr. Hannah I. Evans
146 E 11th St, Denver 80204
(303) 629-0690

Health and Hospitals Mental Health
Program
W 8th Ave and Cherokee
Denver 80204
(303) 893-7001

National Center for the Prevention and
Treatment of Child Abuse and Neglect
1205 Oneida St, Denver 80220
(303) 321-3963

Rape Crisis Program
Denver General Hospital
7th and Cherokee, Denver 80204
(303) 893-6000

Victim Support Group
Park East Mental Health Center
P.O. Box 18L, Denver 80218
(303) 320-6840

Victim Witness Project
Denver District Attorney's Office
Westside Court Bldg
924 W Colfax Ave, Denver 80204
(303) 575-3229

York Street Center for Victims of
Crime and Family Violence
1632 York St, Denver 80206
(303) 321-8191 (*rape hotline*);
(303) 333-6626 (*family violence*);
(303) 388-0834 (*office*)

Rape Intervention Team
c/o Community Hospital
3801 N Main Ave, Durango 81301
(303) 259-1110

Community Crisis and Information
Center
626 Remington St, Fort Collins 80524
(303) 493-3888

Rape Crisis Team
525 W Oak, Fort Collins 80521
(303) 221-2100, ext 380

Rape Crisis Center
1059 Rood, Grand Junction 81501
(303) 243-0190

Weld County Rape Crisis Team
National Organization for Women
Box 124, 1201 A St, Greeley 80631
(303) 352-4551

Weld Mental Health Center
1306 11th Ave, Greeley 80631
(303) 353-3686

Midwestern Colorado Mental Health
Center
P.O. Box 1208, Montrose 81401
(303) 249-9694

Adams County Rape Task Force
c/o Jan Strauss
10280 N Huron, Northglenn 80221
(303) 451-1173

Center for Victims of Violence
801 N Santa Fe Ave, Pueblo 81003
(303) 544-3131

Sexual Assault Program
Lutheran Medical Center
8300 W 38th Ave, Wheatridge 80033
(303) 425-4500, ext 2089

Connecticut

Rape Crisis Service
YWCA of Greater Bridgeport
1862 E Main St, Bridgeport 06610
(203) 333-2233 (*hotline*);
(203) 334-6154 (*office*)

Womanshare, Inc.
c/o Greenwich YWCA
Greenwich 06830
(203) 867-6501

Neighborhood Women Against Rape
P.O. Box 14272, Hartford 06114
(203) 525-1163, ext 205

Sexual Assault Crisis Service/YWCA
135 Broad St, Hartford 06105
(203) 522-6666 (*hotline*);
(203) 525-1163, ext 205 (*office*)

Sex Crimes Unit
Connecticut State Police
294 Colony St, Meriden 06450
(203) 238-6575

SAFE, Middletown Women and Men
Against Sexual Assault
Community Health Center
635 Main St, Middletown 06457
(203) 346-7233

Milford Rape Crisis Center
P.O. Box 521, Milford 06460
(203) 878-1212

Rape Counseling Team
Yale–New Haven Hospital
789 Howard Ave, New Haven 06510
(203) 436-1960

Rape Crisis Center
148 Orange St, New Haven 06510
(203) 397-2273

Sex Offender Program
Connecticut Correctional Institution—
Somers
P.O. Box 100, Somers 06071
(203) 749-8391, ext 36

Rape Crisis Service of Stamford
322 Main St, Stamford 06820
(203) 329-2929 (*hotline*);
(203) 348-9346 (*office*)

Rape Crisis Counseling Center
University of Connecticut
28 Whitney Rd, Box U–118
Storrs 06268
(203) 423-9595 (*hotline*);
(203) 486-4738 (*office*)

Sexual Assault Crisis Service of the
Central Naugatuck Valley, Inc.
YWCA
80 Prospect St, Waterbury 06702
(203) 753-3613

Delaware

Support Group for Victims of Sexual
Offense (S.O.S.)
Laurel Hall, University of Delaware
Newark 19711
(302) 738-2226 (*hotline*);
(302) 738-1202 (*office*)

Rape Crisis Center of Wilmington
P.O. Box 1507, Wilmington 19899
(302) 658-5011

**District of Columbia
(Washington, DC)**

American Bar Association
Criminal Justice Section
1800 M St, NW, Washington 20036
(202) 331-2260

Child Sexual Abuse Program
Children's Hospital National Medical
Center
111 Michigan Ave, NW
Washington 20010
(202) 745-5682

FACT Hotline (Families and Children
in Trouble)
Family Stress Services of the District of
Columbia
Box C, 1690 36th St, NW
Washington 20007
(202) 628-3228 (*hotline*);
(202) 965-1900 (*office*)

Feminist Alliance Against Rape
(FAAR)
P.O. Box 21033, Washington 20009
(202) 543-5580

National Women's Health Network
2025 I St, NW, Suite 105
Washington 20006
(202) 223-6887

Sexual Assault Follow Up Program
Department of Human Resources
DC General Hospital
19th and C Sts, SE, Washington 20003
(202) 727-4906

Sexual Assault Program
Women's Medical Center of
Washington, DC
1712 I St, NW, Suite 704
Washington 20006
(202) 298-9227; (202) 298-6655
(*teletype for hearing-impaired*)

Sexual Offense Branch
Metropolitan Police Department
300 Indiana Ave, NW
Washington 20001
(202) 727-4151

Women's Equity Action League
805 15th St, NW, Washington 20005
(202) 638-4560

Florida

Mentally Disordered Sex Offender Unit
Forensic Service
Florida State Hospital
P.O. Box 1000, Chattahoochee 32324
(904) 663-7201 or 663-7286

Victim Advocate Program and
Investigation Unit
125 E Orange Ave
Daytona Beach 32014
(904) 258-7000

Broward County Witness Liaison
Office
Broward County Courthouse, Suite 510
201 SE 6th St, Fort Lauderdale 33301
(305) 765-4572

Victim Advocate Office
Fort Lauderdale Police Department
1300 W Broward Blvd
Fort Lauderdale 33312
(305) 761-2143

Rape Victim Advocate Program
Office of the State Attorney
8th Judicial Circuit
P.O. Box 1437, Gainesville 32602
(904) 377-6888 (*hotline*);
(904) 374-3604 (*office*)

Dr. Geraldine Boozer Rehabilitation
Program for Sex Offenders
South Florida State Hospital
1000 SW 84th Ave, Hollywood 33023
(305) 963-6040 (*hotline*);
(305) 983-4321 (*office*)

Hubbard House
222 W Duval, Jacksonville 32206
(904) 354-3114

Police Public Services
Office of the Sheriff
501 E Bay St, Jacksonville 32202
(904) 633-4444

Rape Crisis Center
Emergency Treatment Unit
Community Mental Health Center
University Hospital
655 W 8th St, Jacksonville 32209
(904) 358-3272, ext 2533

Rape Crisis Center of Polk County,
Inc.
201½ E Lemon St, Rm 28
Lakeland 33801
(813) 299-5858 (*hotline*);
(813) 683-7373 (*office*)

Dade County Victims Advocate
Program
1515 NW 7th St, Suite 112
Miami 33125
(305) 358-4357 (*hotline*);
(305) 547-7933 (*office*)

Rape Treatment Center
1611 NW 12th Ave, Miami 33136
(305) 325-6949

Creative Services
Rape Crisis—Spouse Abuse
721 NE 3rd St, Ocala 32670
(904) 622-8495

Rape Crisis Intervention Program
Orlando Regional Medical Center
1414 S Kuhl Ave, Orlando 32802
(305) 841-5111

Orange County Victim Advocate/
Education Program
Orange County Sheriff's Department
1 N Court St, Orlando 32801
(305) 656-6006

Rape Crisis Center of West Florida
YWCA
1417 N 12th Ave, Pensacola 32503
(904) 433-7273

SPARCC—Safe Place and Rape Crisis
Center of Sarasota, Inc.
3800 S Tamiami Trail, Sarasota 33579
(813) 365-1976 (*hotline*);
(813) 365-0208 (*office*)

Help Stop Crime!
The Capitol
Tallahassee 32301
(904) 488-5804

Women's Center of Tampa, Inc.
609 DeLeon St, Tampa 33606
(813) 251-8629

Sexual Assault Assistance Project
Pan-Am Bldg, Rm 308
307 N Dixie Hwy
West Palm Beach 33401
(305) 833-7273 (*hotline*);
(305) 837-2073 (*office*)

Georgia

Rape Crisis Center
Grady Memorial Hospital
80 Butler St, SE, Atlanta 30303
(404) 588-4861

Augusta Rape Crisis Line
P.O. Box 3474, Hill Station
Augusta 30904
(404) 724-5200

Carroll County Crisis Intervention
Center
827 Maple St, Carrollton 30117
(404) 834-3326

North Central Georgia Mental Health
Center
1407 Burleyson St, Dalton 30720
(404) 259-2305

Central Georgia Comprehensive
Community Mental Health/Mental
Retardation Center
Consultation and Education Unit
420 College St, Macon 31201
(912) 746-1551

Clayton County Community Mental
Health Center
15 SW Upper Riverdale Rd,
Riverdale 30724
(404) 471-4357

Rape Crisis Center of the Coastal
Empire, Inc.
P.O. Box 8492, Savannah 31412
(912) 233-7273

Hawaii

Alternatives for Women Program
Diamond Head Mental Health Center
550 Makapuu Ave, Honolulu 96816
(808) 737-5465

Sex Abuse Treatment Center
Kapiolani Children's Medical Center
1319 Punahou St, Honolulu 96826
(808) 524-7273 (*hotline*);
(808) 947-8589 (*office*)

Windward Oahu Community Mental
Health Center
45-691 Keaahala Rd, Kaneohe 96744
(808) 247-2148

Idaho

Rape Crisis Alliance
720 Washington St, Boise 83702
(208) 345-7273

Region III Mental Health Center
107 Poplar, P.O. Box 988
Caldwell 83605
(208) 454-0421

Women's Center
University of Idaho
Moscow 83843
(208) 885-6616

Rape Crisis Center of Canyon County
1417 Second St S, Nampa 83651
(208) 467-7112

Rape Crisis Team
Women's Advocates
454 N Garfield, Pocatello 83201
(208) 232-9169

Magic Valley Rape Crisis Center
Burley/Rupert Center
Box 624, Rupert 83350
(208) 436-3406 (*hotline*);
(208) 436-5711, ext 27 (*office*)

Magic Valley Rape Crisis Center
Twin Falls Center
P.O. Box 886, Twin Falls 83301
(208) 734-7273

Illinois

Family Support Center
169 N Fourth St, Aurora 60505
(312) 897-1003

Call for Help—Rape Team
7623 (Rear) W Main St
Belleville 62223
(618) 397-0963

Fulton County Women's Crisis Service,
Inc.
111 N Ave A, Canton 61520
(309) 647-2466

Burnham Hospital Emergency
Department
407 S 4th St, Champaign 61820
(217) 337-2533

American Society of Clinical
Pathologists
2100 W Harrison St, Chicago 60612
(312) 738-1336

Chicago Counseling and Psychotherapy
Center
5711 S Woodlawn Ave, Chicago 60637
(312) 684-1800

Chicago Women Against Rape
Loop YWCA—Women's Services
37 S Wabash, Chicago 60603
(312) 372-6600, ext 61

Citizens' Committee for Victim
Assistance
11 S LaSalle St, Suite 2812
Chicago 60603
(312) 762-0377

Code R Program
Billings Hospital of the University of
Chicago Hospitals and Clinics
Box 215, 950 E 59th St, Chicago 60637
(312) 947-5140

Department of Emergency Medicine
Billings Hospital of the University of
Chicago Hospitals and Clinics
950 E 59th St, Chicago 60637
(312) 947-6735

Illinois Crime Victims Compensation
Program
188 W Randolph St, Suite 2200
Chicago 60601
(312) 793-2585

Information and Referral
Illinois Department of Children and
Family Services
1026 S Damen, Chicago 60612
(312) 793-2100

Law Enforcement Project
South East Chicago Commission
1400 F 53rd St, Chicago 60615
(312) 324-6926

Metro-Help, Inc.
2210 N Halsted St, Chicago 60614
(312) 929-5150

Planned Parenthood—Chicago Area
55 E Jackson Blvd, Chicago 60604
(312) 322-4219

PUSH for Excellence
Reproductive Health Department
930 E 50th St, Chicago 60615
(312) 373-3366

Rape Victim Advocate Program
Rush-Presbyterian-St. Luke's Hospital
1725 W Harrison, Chicago 60612
(312) 942-5000

Rape Victim Advocates
P.O. Box 11537, Chicago 60611
(312) 883-5688

Victim/Witness Project
National District Attorneys Association
666 N Lakeshore Dr, Suite 1432
Chicago 60611
(312) 944-4610

Women In Crisis Can Act, Inc.
(WICCA)
1628A W Belmont, Chicago 60657
(312) 528-3303

Women Services
Northeastern Illinois University
5500 N St. Louis Ave, Office B–114
Chicago 60625
(312) 583-4050, ext 375 or 376

Victim/Witness Advocate Program
2 South St, Danville 61832
(217) 442-4466

Citizens Against Rape
436 N Main St, Decatur 62521
(217) 429-7444

Quad-Cities Training Center
3010 4th Ave, East Moline 61244
(309) 755-3428

National Coalition Against Sexual
Assault (NCASA)
Pam Klein, President
P.O. Box 154, Edwardsville 62026
(618) 692-2197

Rape and Sexual Abuse Care Center
Southern Illinois University at
Edwardsville
166 Bluff Rd, P.O. Box 154
Edwardsville 62026
(618) 692-2197

Crisis Intervention and Referral Service
Evanston Hospital
2650 Ridge Ave, Evanston 60201
(312) 492-6500

Social Service Department
St. Francis Hospital
355 Ridge Ave, Evanston 60202
(312) 492-2230

Student Health Service
Gynecology Department
Northwestern University
633 Emerson St, Evanston 60201
(312) 869-8100, ext 60

The Hope Clinic for Women, Ltd.
1602 21st St, Granite City 62040
(618) 451-5722

Will County Rape Crisis Center
P.O. Box 354, Joliet 60435
(815) 722-3344 (*hotline*);
(815) 744-5280 (*office*)

Dupage Women Against Rape
(DWAR)
1 S Park, Lombard 60148
(312) 495-3927 (*hotline*);
(312) 629-0170 (*office*)

Society for the Preservation of Human
Dignity
P.O. Box 574, Palatine 60067
(312) 359-4919

Committee on Abuse and Rape:
Emergency Services
(YW C.A.R.E.S.)
South Suburban Area YWCA
300 Plaza, Park Forest 60466
(312) 748-5669 (*hotline*);
(312) 748-5660; 748-5672 (*office*)

Northwest Action Against Rape
P.O. Box 508, Prairie View 60069
(312) 398-0727

Comprehensive Community Mental
Health Center of Rock Island and
Mercer Counties
2701 17th St, Rock Island 61201
(309) 793-1000

Rape/Sexual Assault Counseling
Center of Scott and Rock Island
Counties
1829 2nd Ave, Rock Island 61201
(309) 786-0090

Rockford Rape Counseling Center, Inc.
P.O. Box 4027, Rockford 61110
(815) 964-4044 (*hotline*);
(815) 962-3268 (*office*)

Division of Emergency Medical
Services and Highway Safety
Department of Public Health
525 W Jefferson, Springfield 62761
(217) 785-2080

Illinois House of Representatives Rape
Study Committee
K–3, William Stratton Bldg
Springfield 62706
(217) 782-8402; (312) 676-2437

Rape Information and Counseling
Service (RICS)
P.O. Box 2211, Springfield 62705
(217) 753-8081 (*hotline*);
(217) 753-0133 (*office*)

Western Springs Police Department
740 Hillgrove Ave
Western Springs 60558
(312) 246-8540

Indiana

Center for Mental Health
2020 Brown St, P.O. Box 1258
Anderson 46015
(317) 649-8161

Women's Alternatives, Inc.
P.O. Box 2769, Anderson 46011
(317) 649-5211

Quinco Consulting Center
Rape and Battered Spouse Crises Line
2075 Lincoln Park Dr, P.O. Box 1143
Columbus 47201
(812) 376-7273 (*hotline*);
(800) 832-5442 (*Indiana only*)

SUPPORT
YWCA Women's Resource Center
122 W Lexington Ave, Elkhart 46514
(219) 293-8671

Citizens Against Rape in Evansville
(C.A.R.E.)
Deaconess Hospital
600 Mary St, Evansville 47713
(812) 425-4355

Southwestern Indiana Mental Health
Center, Inc.
415 Mulberry St, Evansville 47713
(812) 423-7791

Allen County Victim Assistance
Program
12535 Lima Rd, Fort Wayne 46808
(219) 423-7924

Rape Crisis Center, Inc.
P.O. Box 5367, Fort Wayne 46805
(219) 426-7273

Rape Information, Education and
Referral
Mental Health Center
909 E State Blvd, Fort Wayne 46805
(219) 482-9111

Calumet Women United Against Rape
P.O. Box 2617, Gary 46403
(219) 937-0450, 980-4207 and
769-3141 (*local hotlines*)

Adult and Child Mental Health Center
5142 Madison Ave, Indianapolis 46227
(317) 788-9506

Community Education Crime
Prevention Program
Indiana State Board of Health
1330 E Michigan St
Indianapolis 46206
(317) 633-0294

Crisis and Suicide Intervention Service
Mental Health Association
1433 N Meridian St, Rm 202
Indianapolis 46202
(317) 632-7575

Crisis Intervention Service
Gallahue Mental Health Center
Community Hospital of Indianapolis,
Inc.
1500 N Ritter Ave, Indianapolis 46219
(317) 353-5947 (*hotline*);
(317) 353-5457 (*emergency room*);
(317) 353-5931 (*office*)

Crisis Intervention Unit
Midtown Community Mental Health
Center
Wishard Memorial Hospital
1001 W 10th St, Indianapolis 46202
(317) 630-7791

Family Service Association
615 N Alabama St, Indianapolis 46204
(317) 634-6341

Indiana Counseling and Pastoral Care
Center
1717 W 86th St, #130
Indianapolis 46260
(317) 257-3141

Marion County Victim Advocate
Program, Inc.
4602 Thornleigh Dr
Indianapolis 46226
(317) 545-1116

Victim Assistance Program
Indianapolis Police Department
50 N Alabama St, Rm E144
Indianapolis 46204
(317) 633-7775

Public Awareness Against Rape
(P.A.A.R.)
1319 Missouri Ave
Jeffersonville 47150
(812) 283-7227 (*hotline*);
(812) 283-4491 (*office*)

Rape Crisis Intervention Team
Community Mental Health Center
285 Bielby Rd, Lawrenceburg 47025
(812) 537-1302

Women's Committee on Sex Offense
Sex Offense Staff (S.O.S.)
P.O. Box 931, South Bend 46624
(219) 232-3344 (*hotline*);
(219) 234-0061, ext 210 (*office*)

Katherine Hamilton Mental Health
Center, Inc.
2931 Ohio Blvd, Terre Haute 47803
(812) 235-6021 or 232-1181

Lifeline
679 Ohio St, Terre Haute 47807
(812) 235-8333 (*hotline*);
(812) 238-2620 (*office*)

Bloomington Organization for Abused
Women, Inc.
Community Shelter for Abused Women
RR 1, Unionville 47468
(812) 339-3110 (*shelter business
phone*)

Comprehensive Community Mental
Health Center—Rape Crisis Center
520 S 7th St, Vincennes 47591
(812) 885-3291

Protective Services for Sexual Assault
Otis R. Bowen Center for Human
Services
850 N Harrison St, Warsaw 46580
(219) 267-7169

Iowa

Story County Sexual Assault Care
Center
P.O. Box 1150, ISU Station
Ames 50010
(515) 292-1101

Rape/Sexual Assault Counseling
Center of Scott and Rock Island
Counties
Bettendorf Bank Bldg
Bettendorf 52722
(319) 359-4211

Rape Crisis Services—YWCA
318 5th St, SE, Cedar Rapids 52401
(319) 398-3955 (*hotline*);
(319) 365-1458 (*YWCA*)

Gateway YWCA: Women's Resource
Center
317 7th Ave S, Clinton 52732
(319) 243-3611 (*hotline*);
(319) 242-2118 (*office*)

Rape/Sexual Assault Victim Advocates
720 S 17th St, Fort Dodge 50501
(515) 573-8000

Rape Victim Advocacy Program
130 N Madison St, Iowa City 52240
(319) 338-4800

Kansas

Hays Rape Crisis Center
Department of Sociology
Fort Hays State University
Hays 67601
(913) 628-1041

High Plains Comprehensive
Community Mental Health Center
208 E 7th St, Hays 67601
(913) 628-2871

Rape Crisis Program
Southeast Kansas Mental Health
Center
1106 59th St, Humboldt 66748
(316) 473-2241

Reno County Rape Center
P.O. Box 2062, Hutchinson 67501
(316) 663-2522

Junction City–Geary County Rape
Crisis Team
Box 490, Junction City 66441
(913) 238-4131

Police Public Education
No. 1 Civic Center Plaza
Kansas City 66101
(913) 371-2000, ext 507

Douglas County Rape Victim Support
Service, Inc.
1035 Pennsylvania, Lawrence 66044
(913) 841-2345 (*hotline*);
(913) 843-8985 (*office*)

Center for Student Development
Caroline F. Paine, Assistant Dean
Kansas State University
Holtz Hall, Manhattan 66506
(913) 532-6432

North Central Kansas Guidance Center
320 Sunset, Manhattan 66502
(913) 539-5337

Pawnee Comprehensive Mental Health
Center
215 Southwind Place
Manhattan 66502
(913) 539-5337 (*emergency no. for
Clay, Riley, Pottowatomie, Marshall
and Geary Counties*);
(913) 243-1094 (*emergency no. for
Cloud, Washington, Jewell, Mitchell
and Republic Counties*);
(913) 776-1050 (*office*)

Regional Crisis Center for Victims of
Family Abuse or Rape
P.O. Box 164, Manhattan 66502
(913) 539-2785

Johnson County Mental Health Center
6000 Lamar Ave, Mission 66202
(913) 384-1100, ext 350

Can Help
P.O. Box 1364, Topeka 66601
(913) 295-8499

South Sedgwick County Comprehensive
Community Mental Health Center
3620 E Sunnybrook St, Wichita 67210
(316) 685-0201

Wichita Area Rape Center, Inc.
1801 E 10th St, Wichita 67214
(316) 263-3002 (*hotline*);
(316) 263-0185 (*office*)

Kentucky

Lansdowne Mental Health Center—
Emergency Service
2162 Greenup Ave, Ashland 41101
(606) 324-1141

Cumberland River Comprehensive Care
Center
American Greeting Road
P.O. Box 568, Corbin 40701
(606) 528-7010

Division for Mental Health
Bureau for Health Services
Department for Human Resources
275 E Main St, Frankfort 40621
(502) 564-4448

Cumberland River Comprehensive Care
Center
Martins Fork Rd, Harlan 40831
(606) 573-1624

Lexington Rape Crisis Center
P.O. Box 1603, Lexington 40592
(606) 253-2511

Hikes Point Mental Health Center—
Area C
3717 Taylorsville Rd, Louisville 40220
(502) 459-5166

Investigation of Sex Crimes Seminar
Southern Police Institute
School of Police Administration
University of Louisville
Louisville 40208
(502) 588-6561

National Crime Prevention Institute
School of Police Administration
University of Louisville, Shelby
Campus
Louisville 40222
(800) 626-2888 (toll-free)

Okolona Mental Health Center—
Area C
7919 Preston Hwy, Louisville 40219
(502) 968-7121

Project F.I.N.D. (Families Involved in
New Directions)
224 E Broadway, Louisville 40202
(502) 589-8641

R.A.P.E. Relief Center
604 S 3rd St, Louisville 40202
(502) 581-7273

Pennyroyal Mental Health Center
1303 W Noel, Madisonville 42431
(502) 821-8874

Women's Crisis Center of Northern
Kentucky
321 York St, Newport 41071
(606) 491-3335

Green River Comprehensive Care
Center Crisis Line—Rape Victim
Services Project
233 W 9th St, Owensboro 42301
(502) 684-9466;
(800) 482-1972 (toll-free number in
Kentucky)

Community Health Centers of Western
Kentucky, Region I
1530 Lone Oak Rd, P.O. Box 1502
Paducah 42001
(800) 592-3980 (toll-free hotline);
(502) 442-7121 (office)

Bullitt County Center—Area C
Third and Beech Sts
Shepherdsville 40165
(502) 957-2498

Region XIV Rape Relief Services
Region XIV Community Mental
Health Services
324 Cundiff Square Downtown,
Somerset 42501
(800) 442-7867 (toll-free hotline);
(606) 678-4493 or 679-1137 (office)

Spencer County Center—Area C
Main St, Taylorsville 40071
(502) 477-2577

Louisiana

Work Against Rape—Sexual Assault
Care Service/HELPLINE
1407 Murray St, #204
Alexandria 71301
(318) 445-4357 (hotline);
(318) 445-2022 (office)

Stop Rape Crisis Center
East Baton Rouge Parish District
Attorney's Office
215 St Louis St, #307
Baton Rouge 70801
(504) 389-3456

Charity Hospital of Louisiana at
New Orleans
1532 Tulane Ave
New Orleans 70140
(504) 568-2835

New Orleans Child Protection Center
8000 Forshey St, New Orleans 70125
(504) 483-4911 (hotline);
(504) 483-4920 (Administrator)

Orleans Parish Coroner's Office
2700 Tulane Ave
New Orleans 70119
(504) 586-4061

YWCA Rape Crisis Service
601 S Jefferson Davis Pkwy
New Orleans 70119
(504) 821-6000 (*hotline*);
(504) 488-2693 (*office*)

Women's Resource Center of
the YWCA
710 Travis St, Shreveport 71101
(318) 222-0556 (*hotline*);
(318) 222-2116 (*office*)

Maine

The Rape Crisis Center of Greater
Portland
193 Middle St, Portland 04101
(207) 774-3613 (*hotline*);
(207) 774-4305 (*office*)

Maryland

Anne Arundel County Sexual Offense
Crisis Center
62 Cathedral St, Annapolis 21401
(301) 263-0330

Baltimore Center for Victims of Sexual
Assault
128 W Franklin St, Baltimore 21201
(301) 366-7273

Division of Adolescent Medicine
University of Maryland Hospital
22 S Green St, Rm 8-1159
Baltimore 21201
(301) 528-6495 or 528-5400

Maryland Commission for Women
1100 N Eutaw St, Baltimore 21201
(301) 383-5608

Sex Offense Task Force
Baltimore City State's Attorney's
Office
Criminal Courts Bldg, Rm 221
Baltimore 21202
(301) 396-5040

Sex Offense Unit
Criminal Investigation Division
Baltimore Police Department
601 E Fayette St, Baltimore 21202
(301) 396-2342

Sexually Assaulted People Program
Baltimore City Hospitals
4940 Eastern Ave, Baltimore 21224
(301) 396-9383

Community Crisis Center
Sexual Assault Services
4910 Auburn Ave, Bethesda 20014
(301) 656-9449 (*hotline*);
(301) 656-9526 (*office*)

Prince George's County Sexual Assault
Center
Prince George's General Hospital
and Medical Center
Hospital Dr, Cheverly 20785
(301) 341-4942 (*hotline*);
(301) 341-2005 (*office*)

Women's Crisis Hotline
University of Maryland Health Center
Rm 3114
College Park 20742
(301) 454-4616 or 454-4617

Howard County Rape Crisis Center
P.O. Box 201, Columbia 21045
(301) 997-3292 (*hotline*);
(301) 997-2502 (*office*)

Anne Arundel County Commission for
Women
2972 Solomons Island Rd
Edgewater 21037
(301) 956-4200

International Association of Chiefs
of Police
11 Firstfield Rd, Gaithersburg 20760
(301) 948-0922

Montgomery County Hotline
c/o MHAMC
10920 Connecticut Ave
Kensington 20795
(301) 949-6603

Maryland Police Training Commission
7 Church La, Pikesville 21043
(301) 484-6464

Holy Cross Hospital Emergency
Service
1500 Forest Glen Rd
Silver Spring 20910
(301) 565-1225

Prince George's County Commission
for Women
County Administration Bldg
Rm 1091
Upper Marlboro 20870
(301) 952-3383

Massachusetts

Counselors/Advocates Against Rape
40 Everywoman's Center
Wilder Hall
University of Massachusetts
Amherst 01003
(413) 545-0800 (*hotline*);
(413) 545-0883 (*office*)

Victim/Witness Assistance Project
First District Court
Barnstable County Complex
Barnstable 02630
(617) 362-2511, ext 410

Criminal Victimology
Consultants, Inc.
20A Dartmouth St, Boston 02116
(617) 482-3663

Emergency Services
Peter Bent Brigham Hospital
721 Huntington Ave, Boston 02115
(617) 732-6027

Project Place
32 Rutland St, Boston 02118
(617) 267-9150 (*hotline*);
(617) 262-3740 (*office*)

Rape Crisis Intervention Program
Beth Israel Hospital
330 Brookline Ave, Boston 02215
(617) 735-3337 (*emergency*);
(617) 735-4645 (*information*)

Rape Investigation Unit
Boston Police Department
154 Berkeley St, Boston 02116
(617) 247-4400 or 247-4520

Rape Task Force
Boston Commission to Improve the
Status of Women
Boston City Hall, Rm 603
Boston 02201
(617) 725-4496

Victim/Witness Assistance Project
Suffolk County District
Attorney's Office
Boston Municipal Court, Rm 273
Pemberton Square, Boston 02108
(617) 725-8727

Massachusetts Treatment Center
Box 554, Bridgewater 02324
(617) 697-8161

Alliance Against Sexual Coercion
P.O. Box 385, Cambridge 02139
(617) 482-0329

Boston Area Rape Crisis Center
Women's Center
46 Pleasant St, Cambridge 02139
(617) 492-7273

Francis A. Pisani Academy
Cambridge Police Department
1493 Cambridge St
Cambridge 02119
(617) 864-0604

Victim/Witness Program
40 Thorndike St, Rm 13-11
Cambridge 02167
(617) 494-4430

Boston College Department of
Continuing Education
Cushing Hall, Rm 238
Chestnut Hill 02167
(617) 969-0100, ext 4256 or 4257

Norfolk County Rape Unit
District Attorney's Office
618 High St, Dedham 02026
(617) 326-1600

Mid Cape Rape Crisis Unit
76 Enterprise Rd, Hyannis 02601
(617) 771-1080

Women's Resource Center
Greater Lawrence YWCA
38 Lawrence St, Lawrence 01840
(617) 685-2481

Rape Crisis Intervention Services
Greater Lynn Community Mental
Health Program
Union Hospital, 500 Lynnfield St
Lynn 01904
(617) 595-7273

Newton Wellesley Hospital
Washington St
Newton Lower Falls 02162
(617) 964-2800, ext 481 or 291

Franklin Hampshire County
Community Mental Health Center
50 Pleasant St, Box 625
Northhampton 01060
(413) 586-5555 (*hotline*);
(413) 586-1257 (*office*)

South Shore Hospital
South Weymouth 02190
(617) 337-7011

Hampden County District Attorney's
Victim/Witness Support Program
50 State St, Springfield 01103
(413) 781-8100, ext 2026

Hotline to End Rape and Abuse
(HERA)
26 Howard St, Springfield 01105
(413) 733-2561

Rape Crisis Program
162 Chandler St, Worchester 01609
(617) 799-5700 (*hotline*);
(617) 756-4354 (*office*)

Michigan

Assault Crisis Center
4009 Washtenaw Rd
Ann Arbor 48104
(313) 994-1616 (*hotline*);
(313) 971-9780 (*office*)

Women's Crisis Center
211½ N 4th Ave, Ann Arbor 48107
(313) 995-9100 (*hotline*);
(313) 761-9475 (*office*)

Bay County Women's Center for Rape
and Assault
P.O. Box 646, Bay City 48707
(517) 893-4551

Cass Corridor Safety for
Seniors Project
3150 2nd Ave, Detroit 48201
(313) 224-1225

Detroit Central City Community
Mental Health Center
Consultation and Education
10 Peterboro St, Detroit 48201
(313) 831-3160

Rape Counseling Center
Detroit Police Department
1326 St. Antoine, Rm 828
Detroit 48207
(313) 224-4487 (*day hotline*);
(313) 224-0550 (*night hotline*);
(313) 963-4649 (*office*)

Victim/Witness Assistance Program
Wayne County Prosecuting Attorney's
Office
1441 St. Antoine, Detroit 48226
(313) 224-5800

Sexual Assault Counseling of The
Listening Ear
547½ E Grand River Ave
East Lansing 48823
(517) 337-1717

Sexual Assault Crisis Center
YWCA
310 E 3rd St, Flint 48502
(313) 767-2662

Spouse Abuse/ Rape Program of the
Center for Women in Transition
834 Grant St, Grand Haven 49401
(616) 842-4357 (*northern county
hotline*);
(616) 396-4357 (*southern county
hotline*);
(616) 458-4357 (*eastern county
hotline*);
(616) 842-6310 (*office*)

Rape Crisis Team
750 Cherry, SE, Grand Rapids 49503
(616) 774-3535

Rape/Assault Counseling
2904 Francis St, Jackson 49203
(517) 783-2671 (*hotline*);
(517) 787-9433 (*office*)

Bronson Hospital Trauma and
Emergency Center
252 E Lovell St, Kalamazoo 49007
(616) 383-6386

Kalamazoo Sexual Assault Program
211 S Rose St, Kalamazoo 49006
(616) 565-7199

Macomb County Crisis Center
21885 Dunham Rd, Area 5
Mt. Clemens 48403
(313) 469-6211

Rape/Spouse Assault Crisis Center of
Every Woman's Place, Inc.
29 Strong Ave, Muskegon 49441
(616) 722-3333 (*hotline*);
(616) 726-4493 (*office*)

Oakland Crisis Center for Rape and
Sexual Abuse
YWCA of Pontiac–North Oakland
269 W Huron St, Pontiac 48053
(313) 332-4357 (*hotline*);
(313) 334-0973 (*YWCA*)

St. Clair County Domestic Assault and
Rape Elimination Services Task Force
(D.A.R.E.S.)
2920 Lapeer Ave, Port Huron 48060
(313) 985-7161

Saginaw County Rape Crisis
Center, Inc.
1765 E Genesee St, Saginaw 48601
(517) 755-6565

Women's Resource for the Grand
Traverse Area
918 W Front St, Traverse City 49684
(616) 941-1210

Minnesota

FREEBORN—Mower Crime Victim
Crisis Centers
231 E Clark, Albert Lea 56007
(507) 373-2223

Listening Ear Crisis Center
111 17th Ave E, Alexandria 56308
(612) 763-6638

Victim/Witness Assistance Program
Anoka County Attorney's Office
Anoka County Court House
Anoka 55303
(612) 421-4760, ext 1192

FREEBORN—Mower Crime Victim
Crisis Centers
908 NW 1 Dr, Austin 55912
(507) 437-6680

Beltrami County Sexual Assault
Task Force
Box 1112, Bemidji 56601
(218) 586-2448

Women's Center of Mid-Minnesota,
Inc.
P.O. Box 602, Brainerd 56401
(218) 828-1216

Carver County Program for Victims of
Sexual Assault
Courthouse
600 E 4th, Chaska 55318
(612) 448-2111 (*on call*);
(612) 448-3435, ext 260 (*office*)

Aid to Victims of Sexual Assault
2 E 5th St, Duluth 55805
(218) 727-8538 (*hotline-Duluth*);
(800) 232-1300 (*toll-free*);
(218) 727-4353 (*office*)

Southern Minnesota Crisis Support
Center, Inc.
P.O. Box 214, Fairmont 56031
(507) 235-3456 (*hotline*);
(507) 235-5446 (*office*)

Adult Protection Council
P.O. Box 45, Grand Rapids 55744
(218) 326-8565 (*Nightengale*);
(218) 326-1034 (*information and
referral*)

Dakota County Sexual Assault
Program
Dakota County Government Center
Hwy 55, Hastings 55033
(612) 437-3191, ext 460 or 438

Victim Assistance
410 S 5th, Mankato 56001
(507) 625-9034

Chrysalis, A Center for Women
2104 Stevens Ave S
Minneapolis 55404
(612) 871-2603

Correctional Service of Minnesota
1427 Washington Ave S
Minneapolis 55454
(612) 340-5432

Hennepin County Child Protection
Government Center A–15
300 S 6th St, Minneapolis 55487
(612) 348-3552

Midwest Health Center for Women
825 S 8th St, Minneapolis 55404
(612) 332-2311

Program in Human Sexuality
Department of Family Practice
and Community Health
University of Minnesota
2630 University Ave, SE
Minneapolis 55414
(612) 376-7520

Rape and Sexual Assault Center
1222 W 31st St, Minneapolis 55408
(612) 825-4357

Sexual Assault Services
Hennepin County Attorney's Office
2000 C Government Center
Minneapolis 55405
(612) 348-5397

Northfield Victim Support Program
Box 171, Northfield 55057
(507) 645-5555

Rapeline Program
913 3rd Ave, SE, Rochester 55901
(507) 289-0636 (*hotline*);
(507) 289-3999 (*office*)

Rape Crisis Service
1900 Minnesota Blvd
St. Cloud 56301
(612) 251-4357

Minnesota Crime Victims Reparations
Board
702 American Center Bldg
St. Paul 55101
(612) 296-7080

Minnesota Program for Victims
of Sexual Assault
Minnesota State Department
of Corrections
430 Metro Square Bldg
St. Paul 55101
(612) 296-7084

Sexual Offense Services of
Ramsey County (S.O.S.)
E Kellogg Blvd, St. Paul 55101
(612) 298-5898

Women's Advocates
584 Grand, St. Paul 55102
(612) 227-8284

Intensive Treatment Program for
Sexual Aggressives
Minnesota Security Hospital
2000 S Minnesota Ave
St. Peter 56082
(507) 931-3151

Aid to Victims of Sexual Assault
Courthouse, Rm 16, Virginia 55792
(800) 232-1300 (*toll-free*);
(218) 749-4725

Sexual Assault Crisis Aid
205 Exchange Bldg, Winona 55987
(507) 452-4440

Sexual Abuse Services
Washington County Human
Services, Inc.
8155 Hudson Rd, Woodbury 55042
(612) 738-3600 (*hotline*);
(612) 738-0080 (*office*)

Mississippi

National Organization of Victim
Assistance
P.O. Box 9227, Southern Station
Hattiesburg 39401
(601) 266-4100

Rape Crisis Center
P.O. Box 4174, Jackson 39216
(601) 354-1113 (*hotline*);
(601) 354-5304 (*office*)

Missouri

Life Crisis Services, Inc.
7438 Forsythe, Suite 210
Clayton 63105
(314) 725-2010 (*hotline*);
(314) 721-8500 (*mental health
resource and referral*);
(314) 721-4310 (*office*)

Abuse, Assault, and Rape Crisis Center
(AARCC)
P.O. Box 1827, Columbia 65201
(314) 442-3322 (hotline);
(314) 449-7721 (office)

Association for Women Students
University of Missouri
18 Read Hall, Columbia 65201
(314) 882-2640 or 882-8386

Women's Center
University of Missouri
1 Gentry Hall, Columbia 65201
(314) 882-6621

Division of Family Services
Department of Social Services
Broadway State Office Bldg
Jefferson City 65102
(314) 751-3448

Sexual Assault Treatment Center
St. Lukes Hospital Emergency Room
4400 Wornall Rd, Kansas City 64111
(816) 932-2171

Counter Sexual Assault Task Force
2015 Clay St, St. Joseph 64501
(816) 233-7510

Mental Health Association of St.
Joseph, Inc.
Sisson Bldg, Rm 103
8th and Emond, St. Joseph 64501
(816) 364-2387

Victim/Witness Services
Prosecuting Attorney's Office
Buchanan County Courthouse
St. Joseph 64501
(816) 364-2100 (family guidance
hotline);
(816) 279-6378 (office)

Victim/Witness Sexual Assault Center
St. Joseph's Hospital Emergency Room
10th and Powell, St. Joseph 64501
(816) 364-2100 (hotline);
(816) 271-5000 (office)

Aid to Victims of Crime
607 N Grand Blvd, St. Louis 63103
(314) 531-2597

Crusade Against Crime
1221 Locust St, St. Louis 63103
(314) 231-0425

Sex Crime Section
St. Louis Police Department
1200 Clark Ave, St. Louis 63103
(314) 444-5385

Rape Crisis Assistance, Inc.
430 S Ave, 7th Floor
Springfield 65806
(417) 866-1969, ext 66

Montana

Billings Rape Task Force
1245 N 29th St, Rm 218
Billings 59101
(406) 259-6506

Violence Against Women Crisis Line
and Program
Rape Awareness Program
Helena Woman's Center
146 E 6th Ave, Helena 59601
(406) 443-5353

Kalispell Rape Crisis Line
Box 1385, Kalispell 59901
(406) 755-5067

Women's Place
210 N Higgins, Rm 218
Missoula 59801
(406) 543-7606

Women's Resource Center
University of Montana
Missoula 59812
(406) 243-4153

Nebraska

Nebraska Commission on the
Status of Women
301 Centennial Mall S
P.O. Box 94985
Lincoln 68509
(402) 471-2039 or 471-2144

Rape/Spouse Abuse Crisis Center
1133 H St, Lincoln 68508
(402) 475-7273

Women Against Violence
YWCA
3929 Harney St, Rm 100
Omaha 68131
(402) 345-7273 (hotline);
(402) 342-2748 (office)

Nevada

Community Action Against Rape
749 Veterans Memorial Dr, Rm 150
Las Vegas 89101
(702) 735-1111 (*hotline*);
(702) 385-0471(*office*)

Victim/Witness Center
Clark County District Attorney
302 E Carson Ave, Suite 400
Las Vegas 89101
(702) 386-4204

New Hampshire

INFO-LINE
New Hampshire Social Welfare
Council, Inc.
20 S Main St, Box 1255
Concord 03301
(800) 852-3311 (*New Hampshire only*);
(603) 228-0571

Headrest
14 Church St, Box 221
Lebanon 03766
(603) 448-4400 (*hotline*);
(603) 448-4872 (*office*)

Women's Crisis Line for Rape Victims
and Battered Women
YWCA
72 Concord St, Manchester 03101
(603) 668-2299 (*hotline*);
(603) 625-5785 (*office*)

Rape and Assault Committee for the
Nashua Area, Inc.
10 Prospect St, P.O. Box 217
Nashua 03061
(603) 883-3044 (*hotline*);
(603) 889-5762 (*office*)

Rape and Assault Prevention Program
Portsmouth Police Department
28 Penhallow St, Portsmouth 03801
(603) 436-2145

New Jersey

Women's Crisis Services of Hunterdon
County
Box 217, Annandale 08801
(201) 782-4357

Atlantic County Prosecutor's Office
1625 Atlantic Ave
Atlantic City 08401
(609) 345-6700

Adult Diagnostic and Treatment Center
P.O. Box 190, Avenel 07001
(201) 574-2250

Rape Program
Crisis Intervention Unit
East Orange General Hospital
300 Central Ave, East Orange 07019
(201) 672-9685

Union County Prosecutor's Office
Major Crimes Unit
Elizabethtown Plaza, Elizabeth 07207
(201) 654-3000 (*hotline*);
(201) 527-4500 (*office*)

Hunterdon Medical Center Emergency
Department
Rt 31, Flemington 08822
(201) 782-2121

Sexual Assault Unit
Hunterdon County
Prosecutor's Office
8 Court St, Flemington 08822
(201) 788-1129

Denise N. Kleis
812 Blen Rd, Fort Lee 07024
(201) 943-8322

National Council on Crime and
Delinquency
Continental Plaza
411 Hackensack Ave
Hackensack 07601
(201) 488-0400

Sex Crimes/Child Abuse Unit
Bergen County Prosecutor's Office
Bergen County Courthouse
Hackensack 07601
(201) 646-2300

Supporting the Elimination of Rape,
Violence and
Exploitation (S.E.R.V.E.)
191 Main St, Hackensack 07601
(201) 343-3043

Women's Counseling and
Psychotherapy Service
270 State St, Hackensack 07601
(201) 487-5070

Dr. Marie A. Mastria
146 Berkshire Rd
Hasbrouck Heights 07604

Rape Crisis Intervention Center
Roosevelt Hospital
Box 151, Metuchen 08840
(201) 321-6966

CONTACT of Burlington County
P.O. Box 333, Moorestown 08059
(609) 234-8888, 871-4700 and
267-8500

Women's Crisis Center
56 College Ave
New Brunswick 08904
(201) 828-7273

Sexual Assault Rape Analysis Unit
(S.A.R.A.)
22 Franklin St, Newark 07102
(201) 733-7273

Rape Evaluation and
Sex Crimes Unit
Passaic County Prosecutor's Office
77 Hamilton St, Paterson 07505
(201) 742-4357

YWCA–Women's Resource Center
185 Carroll St, Paterson 07501
(201) 684-6408

Muhlenberg Hospital
Park Ave and Randolph Rd
Plainfield 07060
(201) 668-2000

Emergency Services "Guideline"
Somerset County Community Mental
Health Center
22 N Bridge St, Somerville 08876
(201) 526-4100

John F. Kennedy Memorial Hospital
25 E Laurel Rd, Stratford 08084
(609) 784-4000

Incest Counseling Unit
New Jersey Division of Youth and
Family Services
1901 N Olden Ave, Trenton 08618
(609) 984-6347

New Jersey Division on Women
New Jersey Department of Community
Affairs
363 W State St, Trenton 08625
(800) 322-8092 (toll-free hotline);
(609) 292-8840 (office)

NOW–New Jersey Rape Task Force
NOW Office
32 W Lafayette St, Trenton 08618
(609) 393-7474

Treatment Program for Sex Offenders
State Prison
Trenton 08625
(609) 292-6928

New Mexico

HELPline Rape Crisis Team
Otero County Mental Health
Association
1408 8th St, Alamogordo 88310
(505) 437-8680 (hotline);
(505) 437-7404 (office)

Albuquerque Rape Crisis Center
917 Vassar, NE, Albuquerque 87106
(505) 247-0707 (hotline);
(505) 242-4619 (office)

Alternative House, Inc.
1019 Tijeras, NW, P.O. Box 1280
Albuquerque 87103
(505) 247-0173

Family, Community and Emergency
Medicine Department
University of New Mexico
School of Medicine
620 Camino de Salud, NE
Albuquerque 87131
(505) 277-2165

New Mexico Commission on the Status
of Women
600 2nd NW, Suite 811
Albuquerque 87102
(505) 842-3141

Victim/Witness Assistance Program
Office of the District Attorney
415 Tijeras, NW, Albuquerque 87102
(505) 766-4370

Women's Center
University of New Mexico
1824 Las Lomas, NE
Albuquerque 87106
(505) 277-3716

Artesia Rape Crisis Team
Artesia Council for
Human Services, Inc.
305 S 13th, Artesia 88210
(505) 746-9042 (*hotline*);
(505) 746-6222 (*office*)

Carlsbad Area Rape Crisis Center
Carlsbad Area Counseling and
Resource Center
701 N Canal, Carlsbad 88220
(505) 885-8888 (*hotline*);
(505) 887-0493 (*office*)

Rape Crisis Program
P.O. Box 1132, Deming 88030
Enterprise 333 (*toll-free number*);
(505) 546-2174 (*office*)

Rape Counseling Program
Counseling Services of
Northern New Mexico
816 Los Alamos Hwy
Espanola 87532
(505) 753-6985 (*hotline*);
(505) 753-6583 (*office*)

Center Against Sexual Assault (CASA)
607 E Apache, Farmington 87401
(505) 325-1906 (*hotline*);
(505) 327-9824 (*office*)

Crisis Life Line
McKinley County
Community Mental Health
Box 936, 800 Hospital Dr
Gallup 87301
(505) 722-5200 (*hotline*);
(505) 722-2266 (*office*)

Rape Crisis
Western Valencia County Human
Resources, Inc.
1500 N 3rd St, Grants 87020
(505) 287-8504 (*hotline*);
(505) 287-4680 or 287-2552 (*office*)

Rape Crisis Center
Lea County Crisis Center, Inc.
920 W Broadway, Hobbs 88240
(505) 393-6633 (*hotline*);
(505) 393-3168 (*office*)

Southwest Community
Mental Health Services
1480 N Main St, Las Cruces 88001
(505) 526-3371

Rape Crisis Services
Bridge Crisis Center
113 Bridge St, Las Vegas 87701
(505) 425-6794 (*hotline*);
(505) 425-5872 (*office*)

Area Human Resources Council, Inc.
312 W 4th, Lordsburg 88045
(505) 542-9477

Los Alamos Family Council, Inc.
P.O. Box 488, Los Alamos 87544
(505) 662-4422 (*hotline*);
(505) 662-3264 (*office*)

Roosevelt County Rape Crisis
Advocacy
Mental Health Resources, Inc.
300 E First St, Portales 88130
(800) 432-2159 (*hotline*);
(505) 359-1221 (*office*)

Counseling and Resource Center
139 S 2nd St, Box 1583, Raton 87740
(505) 445-5561

Roswell Rape Crisis Services
Community Counseling and
Resource Center
124 E 4th, Roswell 88201
(505) 622-7600 (*hotline*);
(505) 623-1480 (*office*)

Lincoln County Rape Crisis Program
P.O. Box 2480, Ruidoso 88345
(505) 437-8680 (*hotline*);
(505) 257-5038 (*office*)

Santa Fe Rape Crisis Center, Inc.
839 Harvey Building, Suite B
Paseo de Peralta, Santa Fe 87501
(505) 982-4667

Sexual Crimes Prosecution and
Treatment Program
HED–BHSD, P.O. Box 968
Santa Fe 87503
(505) 827-5271, ext 210

Sexual Offenders/Victim Program
Division of Corrections
Penitentiary of New Mexico
P.O. Box 1059, Santa Fe 87501
(505) 827-2485

Rape Crisis Intervention Program
Area Human Resources Council, Inc.
100 E Market St, P.O. Box 677
Silver City 88061
(505) 538-3488 (hotline);
Enterprise 333 (toll-free number);
(505) 388-4412 (office)

Southwest Mental Health Center—
Socorro
311 McCutcheon, Socorro 87801
(505) 835-2444

Community Against Rape, Inc.
Box 3170, Taos 87571
(505) 758-2910

Southwest Community Mental Health
Services, Inc.
112 Broadway
Truth or Consequences 87901
(505) 894-3097;
(505) 894-2111 (after hours
emergency)

Mental Health Resources, Inc.
P.O. Box 1121, 300 S 2nd
Tucumcari 88401
(505) 461-3013

New York

Rape Crisis Center
56–58 Whitney Ave
Binghamton 13904
(607) 722-4256

Borough Crisis Center
Mayor's Task Force on Rape
Lincoln Hospital
234 E 149th St, Bronx 10451
(212) 579-5326, 579-5327 or
579-5328

Crime Victim Assistance Unit
Bronx District Attorney's Office
215 E 161st St, Rm 4B12
Bronx 10451
(212) 590-2115 or 590-2318

Borough Crisis Center
Mayor's Task Force on Rape
Kings County Hospital
451 Clarkson Ave (C Bldg)
Brooklyn 11203
(212) 735-2424, 735-2425 or
735-2426

Kings County Hospital Rape Victim
Companion Program
Clarkson Ave, Brooklyn 11203
(212) 735-2809 or 270-1750

Anti-Rape Advocacy
Crisis Services, Inc.
3258 Main St, Buffalo 14214
(716) 838-5980

Erie County Medical Center
462 Grider St, Buffalo 14215
(716) 898-3656

Medical Emergency Room
Children's Hospital of Buffalo
219 Bryant St, Buffalo 14222
(716) 878-7480

Planned Parenthood of Buffalo, Inc.
210 Franklin St, Buffalo 14202
(716) 853-1771

Rape Prevention:
Campus and Community
Department of Public Safety
Buffalo State College
1300 Elmwood Ave, 110 Chase Hall
Buffalo 14222
(716) 878-6333

Aid to Women Victims of Violence
YWCA
14 Clayton Ave, Cortland 13045
(607) 756-6363

Victims Information Bureau of Suffolk,
Inc.
501 Route 111, Hauppauge 11787
(516) 360-3606 (hotline);
(516) 360-3730 (office)

Borough Crisis Center
Mayor's Task Force on Rape
Queens Hospital Center
82–68 164th St, Jamaica 11432
(212) 990-3187, 990-3188 or
990-3189

Queens County
Special Victims Bureau
Office of the District Attorney
125–01 Queens Blvd
Kew Gardens 11415
(212) 520-2132

Sex Crimes Unit
Nassau County Police Department
1490 Franklin Ave, Mineola 11791
(516) 535-5240

Ad Hoc Committee on Rape
American Medical Women's
Association
c/o Ms. Lorraine Loesel
1740 Broadway, New York 10019
(212) 586-8683

Association of Junior Leagues, Inc.
825 Third Ave, New York 10022
(212) 355-4380

Borough Crisis Center
Mayor's Task Force on Rape
Harlem Hospital
506 Lenox Ave, New York 10037
(212) 694-8251, 694-8252 or
694-8253

Criminal Justice Center
John Jay College of Criminal Justice
444 W 56th St, New York 10019
(212) 247-1600

Fund for Modern Courts, Inc.
Court Monitoring Project
36 W 44th St, New York 10036
(212) 869-1130

Mayor's Task Force on Rape
Central Office
2 Lafayette St, 3rd Floor
New York 10805
(212) 566-1010

National Board YWCA of the U.S.A.
600 Lexington Ave, New York 10022
(212) 753-4700

New York National Organization
for Women
84 Fifth Ave, Rm 907
New York 10011
(212) 989-7230

Rape Crisis Program
Department of Community Medicine
St. Vincent's Hospital
153 W 11th St, New York 10011
(212) 790-8068;
(212) 790-8000 (evenings, weekends)

Rape Intervention Program
St. Luke's/Roosevelt Hospital Center
419 W 114th St, Rm 522
New York 10025
(212) 870-1875 or 870-1048

Sex Crimes Analysis Unit
New York City Police Department
1 Police Plaza, Rm 1312
New York 10038
(212) 233-3000

Sex Crimes Prosecution Unit
New York County
District Attorney's Office
155 Leonard St, New York 10013
(212) 553-9305

Sexual Behavior Clinic
New York State Psychiatric Institute
722 W 168th St, New York 10032
(212) 568-4000, ext 303 or 357

Victim Services Agency, Inc.—Hotline
2 Lafayette St, New York 10007
(212) 577-7777 (hotline);
(212) 577-7700 (office)

Witness Aid Services Unit
New York County
District Attorney's Office
155 Leonard St, New York 10013
(212) 553-8868

Women's Martial Arts Center
16 W 30th St, New York 10001
(212) 685-4553

Niagara County Task Force on Rape
Niagara Falls Memorial
Medical Center
621 Tenth St, Niagara Falls 14302
(716) 278-4528

Family Crisis Program
Mental Health Clinic
South Nassau Communities Hospital
2485 Oceanside Rd, Oceanside 11572
(516) 764-2600, ext 350

Oneonta Rape Crisis Network
85 Chestnut St, Oneonta 13820
(607) 432-2115

Rape Resources of Clinton County
P.O. Box 44, Plattsburgh 12901
(518) 563-6904

Rape Crisis Service of Planned
Parenthood of
Rochester and Monroe County
24 Windsor St, Rochester 14605
(716) 546-2595

Niagara County
Criminal Justice Board
NCCC, Sanborn 14132
(716) 731-3595

Rape Crisis Service of
Schenectady, Inc.
YWCA
44 Washington Ave
Schenectady 12305
(518) 346-2266

Information and Referral Service of the
Volunteer Center, Inc.
Gridley Bldg, 4th Floor
103 E Water St, Syracuse 13202
(315) 474-7011

Rape Crisis Center of Syracuse, Inc.
304 Seymour St, Syracuse 13204
(315) 422-7273

Victim Witness Assistance Program
Onondaga County Civic Center
12th Floor
Syracuse 13202
(315) 474-7011 (hotline);
(315) 425-3900 or 425-2470 (office)

Bureau of Sex Crimes Analysis and
Crisis Intervention
Westchester County Sheriff's Office
110 Grove St, White Plains 10601
(914) 592-8400 (hotline);
(914) 682-2120 or 682-2119 (office)

Center for Preventive Psychiatry, Inc.
340 Mamaroneck Ave
White Plains 10605
(914) 949-7680

North Carolina

Rape Crisis Center of Asheville
331 College St, Allen Center
Asheville 28801
(704) 255-7576

Rape Crisis Alliance of
Alamance County
Box 652, Burlington 27215
(919) 227-6220

Suicide and Crisis Service of Alamance
County, Inc.
344 Maple Ave, P.O. Box 2573
Burlington 27215
(919) 227-6220

Chapel Hill–Carrboro
Rape Crisis Center
Box 871, Chapel Hill 27514
(919) 967-7273 (hotline);
(919) 929-0471, ext 240 (office)

Emergency Room
Rape Crisis Program
North Carolina Memorial Hospital
Manning Drive, Chapel Hill 27514
(919) 966-4721

Charlotte-Mecklenburg
Rape Crisis Service
P.O. Box 29055, Charlotte 28212
(704) 373-0982

Cabarrus County Rape Crisis Council
P.O. Box 1050, Concord 28025
(704) 788-1130

Durham Rape Crisis Center
P.O. Box 2491, West Durham Station
Durham 27705
(919) 688-4353

North Carolina
Rape Crisis Association
Durham Rape Crisis Center
P.O. Box 2491, West Durham Station
Durham 27705

Gaston County
Rape Crisis Council, Inc.
c/o Sam Snyder
2535 Court Dr, Gastonia 28052
(704) 867-4411

Rape: Action, Prevention, Education
Center, Inc. of Greensboro, NC
314 N Davie St, Greensboro 27401
(919) 273-7273 (*hotline*);
(919) 379-5229 (*office*)

Pitt County Mental Health Center
306 Statonsburg Hwy
Greenville 27834
(919) 752-7151

Rape Victim Companion Program
REAL Crisis Intervention, Inc.
1117 Evans St, Greenville 27834
(919) 758-4357

Vance County Rape Crisis
1740 Maynard St, Henderson 27536
(919) 438-8889

Rape Victim Assistance, Inc.
Family Service Bureau
410 Gatewood Ave, High Point 27260
(919) 431-7273 (*hotline*);
(919) 883-1709 (*family services*)

Southeastern General Hospital
Box 1408, Lumberton 28358
(919) 738-6441

Foothills Rape Crisis Service
Burke County
Human Resource Center
East Parker Rd, Morganton 28655
(704) 433-4200

North Carolina Council on the
Status of Women
526 N Wilmington St, Raleigh 27604
(919) 733-2455

Elizabethann O'Sullivan
Department of Political Science
North Carolina State University
P.O. Box 5305, Raleigh 27650
(919) 737-2481

Rape Crisis Center of Raleigh
P.O. Box 5223, Raleigh 27650
(919) 782-3060

The Rape, Child and Family
Abuse Crisis Council of
Salisbury-Rowan, Inc.
130 Council St, Salisbury 27260
(704) 636-9222 (*hotline*);
(704) 636-4718 (*office*)

Rape and Abuse Prevention Group of
Statesville/Iredell County, Inc.
116 N Kelly St, Statesville 28677
(704) 872-3403

Resources, Education, Assistance,
Counseling, and Housing (R.E.A.C.H.)
P.O. Box 1828, Sylva 28779
(704) 586-6103 (*hotline*);
(704) 586-5031 (*office*)

Crisis Line/Open House
315 Walnut St, Wilmington 28401
(919) 763-3695;
(800) 672-2903 (*toll-free*)

Winston Women
Against Rape/Rape Line
P.O. Box 5980, Winston-Salem 27103
(919) 723-5494;
(919) 724-7911 (*Tele-Med Tape: Rape,
A Crime of Violence Against Women;
ask for tape number 899*)

North Dakota

Rape and Abuse Crisis Center of
Fargo-Moorhead
P.O. Box 1655, Fargo 58102
(701) 293-7273

Grand Forks Rape Crisis Center
118 N 3rd St, Box 1695
Grand Forks 58201
(701) 746-6666 (*hotline*);
(701) 772-8171 (*office*)

Ohio

Akron Rape Crisis Center
St. Paul's Episcopal Church
1361 W Market St, Akron 44313
(216) 434-7273

Witness Assistance Program
209 S High St, Akron 44308
(216) 379-5104

Ashland County Guidance Center
738 Claremont Ave, Ashland 44805

Ashtabula Rape Crisis Center
P.O. Box 521, Ashtabula 44004
(216) 998-2607

Aultman Hospital Association
2600 Sixth St, SW, Canton 44710
(216) 452-9911

Rape Crisis Center
American Red Cross
618 2nd St, NW, Canton 44703
(216) 452-1111

Timken Mercy Medical Center
1320 Timken Mercy Dr, NW
Canton 44708
(216) 489-1000 (*hospital*);
(216) 489-1125 (*Social Service
Department*)

Women Helping Women, Inc.
9th and Walnut Sts, Cincinnati 45202
(513) 381-5610 (*hotline*);
(513) 381-6003 (*office*)

Community Guidance and Human
Services Mental Health Center
3740 Euclid, Cleveland 44115
(216) 431-7774

Witness/Victim Service Center of
Cuyahoga County
Justice Center
1215 W 3rd St, Cleveland 44113
(216) 623-7345 or 623-7399

Rape Prevention Program
Columbus Area Community Mental
Health Center
1515 E Broad St, Columbus 43205
(614) 252-0711

Victim Witness Assistance
Prosecuting Attorney's Office
Franklin County Hall of Justice
369 S High St, Columbus 43215
(614) 462-3886

Women Against Rape
P.O. Box 02084, Columbus 43202
(614) 221-4447 (*hotline*);
(614) 291-9751 (*information*)

Coshocton County Crisis Hotline
224 N Fourth St, Coshocton 43812
(614) 622-3457

EASTWAY Community Mental
Health Center
1040 S Smithville Rd, Dayton 45403
(513) 254-8406

Victim/Witness Division
Montgomery County
Prosecutor's Office
41 N Perry St, Rm 315
Dayton 45402
(513) 223-8085

Townhall II Helpline
225 E College Ave, Kent 44240
(216) 672-4357

Project Women
Rape and Battered Victims
Crisis Center
712½ N Fountain Ave
Springfield 45504
(513) 325-3707

Rape/Domestic Violence Program
Zepf Community
Mental Health Center
2060 Glendale Ave, Toledo 43614
(419) 385-5768

Toledo United Against Rape
P.O. Box 4372, 1723 Broadway
Toledo 43609
(419) 475-0494

Rape Crisis Team of
Trumbull County
P.O. Box 1403, Warren 44483
(216) 393-1565

Muskingum Comprehensive Mental
Health Center
2845 Bell St, Zanesville 43701
(614) 452-8403

Oklahoma

Self-Protection for Women
WH101A, Central State University
Edmond 73034
(405) 341-2980, ext 233

Rape Crisis Team
Northwest Oklahoma Pastoral Care
Association, Inc.
617 S Quincy, P.O. Box 3165
Enid 73701
(405) 234-1111 (*hotline*);
(405) 237-8400 (*office*)

Police Community Relations Division
and Crime Prevention Unit
Norman Police Department
101 E Gray, Norman 73069
(405) 321-1444

Women's Resource Center
207½ E Gray, P.O. Box 474
Norman 73071
(405) 364-9424

Rape Victim Assistance
57th and N Shartel,
Oklahoma City 73118
Mailing Address: P.O. Box 765
Bethany 73008
(405) 521-0234

YWCA Women's Resource Center—
Rape Crisis
135 NW 19th, Oklahoma City 73118
(405) 524-7273 (*hotline*);
(405) 528-5440 (*office*)

Oregon

Rape Crisis Center
P.O. Box 914, 216 SW Madison
Corvallis 97330
(503) 754-0110

Sunflower House: Crisis Intervention
128 SW 9th, Corvallis 97330
(503) 753-1241

Associated Lane Interagency Rape
Team (A.L.I.R.T.)
125 E 8th, Rm 170, Eugene 97401
(503) 687-4478 (*information line only*)

Clackamas County Rape Victim
Advocate Program
1450 S Kaen Rd, Oregon City 97045
(503) 655-8616

Karate for Women
1720 SE 12th St, Portland 97214
(503) 233-7070

Multnomah County Crime Prevention
Unit/Personal Safety
12240 NE Glisan, Portland 97230
(503) 255-7422

Rape Prevention Program
Portland Police Bureau
222 SW Pine St, Rm 425
Portland 97204
(503) 248-4126

Rape Victim Advocate Project
Multnomah County District Attorney
804 Multnomah County Courthouse
Portland 97204
(503) 248-5059

Reed Rape Information and Education
Committee
Reed College
3203 SE Woodstock
Portland 97202
(503) 771-1112

Women's Crisis Service
P.O. Box 851, Salem 97308
(503) 399-7722 (*hotline*);
(503) 378-1572 (*office*)

Pennsylvania

Beaver County Assistance for Victims
of Violence
305 Sharon Grange Rd
Aliquippa 15001
(412) 846-9050 or 728-4462

Rape Crisis Council of Lehigh Valley,
Inc.
P.O. Box 1445, Allentown 18105
(215) 437-6610 or 437-6611

Sexual Assault Volunteer Effort
Altoona Hospital
Howard Ave, Altoona 16601
(814) 946-2141

Center on Rape and Assault (CORA)
P.O. Box 604, Butler 16001
(412) 282-4153

Irene Stacy Community Mental Health
Center
112 Hillvue Dr, Butler 16001
(412) 287-0791

Women In Need, Inc. (WIN)
P.O. Box 25, Chambersburg 17201
(717) 264-4444

Gap

Gap

Victim Witness Assistance Unit
Bucks County Courthouse, 4th Floor
Doylestown 18901
(215) 348-2911, ext 555

Rape Crisis Unit
Clearfield/Jefferson Community
Mental Health Center
102 Hospital Ave, DuBois 15801
(814) 371-1100

Rape Crisis Service
162 E Brown St
East Stroudsburg 18301
(717) 421-4000 (*hotline*);
(717) 424-8306 (*office*)

Erie County Rape Crisis Center
356 E 11th St, Erie 16503
(814) 456-1001 (*hotline*);
(814) 454-3440 or 455-4560 (*office*)

Women Organized Against Rape in
Bucks County
1603 Colonial Dr, Feasterville 19047
Mailing Address: Box 793
Langhorne 19047
(215) 752-3596 (*hotline*);
(215) 348-5664 (*office*)

Women's Services of Westmoreland
County
Bank and Trust Bldg
Greensburg 15601
(412) 836-1122 (*hotline*);
(412) 837-9540 (*office*)

Harrisburg Area Rape Crisis Center
P.O. Box 38, Harrisburg 17108
(717) 238-7273

Pennsylvania Coalition Against Rape
(PCAR)
P.O. Box 64, Harrisburg 17108
(717) 232-6745;
(800) 692-7445 (*WATS line in PA*)

YWCA Women's Help Center
526 Somerset St, Johnstown 15901
(814) 536-5361

Lancaster Rape Aid and Prevention
2324 Wood St, Lancaster 17603
(717) 392-7358

Allegheny County Center for Victims
of Violent Crime
810 Walnut St, McKeesport 15132
(412) 664-0788

Crawford County Rape Crisis
751 Liberty St, Meadville 16335
(814) 724-2732

Delaware County Women Against
Rape, Inc.
P.O. Box 211, Media 19063
(215) 566-4342

Victim Witness Program
Delaware County District Attorney's
Office
County Court House, Media 19063
(215) 891-2875 or 891-2866

Tri-City Impact Task Force
Police Department
2400 Leechburg Rd
New Kensington 15068
(412) 337-3331 (*office*);
(412) 339-7531 (*5:00 pm–9:00 am*)

Witness Notification Program
Montgomery County Courthouse
Norristown 19404
(215) 278-3429

Women Against Rape of Montgomery
County, Inc.
P.O. Box 1179, Norristown 19401
(215) 277-5200

Venango County Rape Crisis Center
107 Center St, Oil City 16301
(814) 677-7273

Adult Out-Patient Services
Consortium Catchment Area #4, Inc.
4700 Westminster Ave
Philadelphia 19131
(215) 878-7100

Joseph J. Peters Institute
112 S 16th St, Philadelphia 19102
(215) 568-6627

Temple University Department
of Security
Watts and Berks Sts
Philadelphia 19122
(215) 787-1234

Victim Counseling Service
Philadelphia Bar Association
425 City Hall Annex
Philadelphia 19107
(215) 563-3030

Victim/Witness Assistance Program
District Attorney's Office
2300 Centre Square W
Philadelphia 19102
(215) 686-8090 or 686-8091;
(215) 686-8201 or 686-8211
(*Rape Prosecution Unit*)

Women Organized Against Rape
1220 Sansom St, Philadelphia 19107
(215) 922-3434 (*hotline*);
(215) 922-7400 (*office*)

Allegheny County Center for Victims
of Violent Crime
406 Jones Law Bldg Annex
Pittsburgh 15219
(412) 355-5764

Medical Social Service
Magee-Women's Hospital
Forbes Ave and Halket St
Pittsburgh 15213

Pittsburgh Action Against Rape
211 S Oakland Ave, Pittsburgh 15213
(412) 765-2731 (*hotline*);
(412) 682-0219 (*office*)

Women's Center and Shelter of Greater
Pittsburgh
616 N Highland Ave
Pittsburgh 15206
(412) 661-6066

People Against Rape
Box 885, Reading 19603
(215) 372-7273 (*hotline*);
(215) 372-8425 (*office*)

Women's Center of Beaver County
175 W Washington St
Rochester 15074
(412) 775-0131

Rape Crisis Program at the Women's
Resource Center
321-315A Bank Towers Bldg
Scranton 18503
(717) 346-4671

Rape Crisis Center of Mercer County
76-C Jefferson Ave, Sharon 16146
(412) 528-2110

Rape-Abuse Services
Centre County Women's Resource
Center, Inc.
103 E Beaver Ave
State College 16801
(814) 234-5050 (*hotline*);
(814) 234-5222 (*information and
referral*)

Rape Counseling Information Service
of Fayette County, Inc.
62 E Church St, Uniontown 15401
(412) 437-3737 (*hotline*);
(412) 437-3738 (*office*)

Rape Crisis Council of Chester County
Box 738, West Chester 19380
(215) 692-7273

Luzerne County Women Organized
Against Rape (W.O.A.R.)
132 S Franklin St
Wilkes-Barre 18701
(717) 823-0765

Wise Options for Women
YWCA
815 W Fourth St
Williamsport 17701
(717) 322-4714

Rape Crisis Center of York
P.O. Box 892, York 17405
(717) 845-3656

Community Outreach Program
Volunteers Against Abuse Center
(VAAC)
Route 68, Zelienople 16063
(412) 452-5710

Puerto Rico

Centro De Ayuda a Victimas de
Violacion
Apartado CH-11321
Caparra Heights Station
Caparra Heights 00922
(809) 765-2285 (*hotline*);
(809) 765-2412 (*office*)

Cayey Mental Health Center
392 Jose De Diego Ave W
Cayey 00633
(809) 738-5049, 738-5020 or
738-2222

Commission for Women's Issues
Edificio Garraton—2nd Floor
1608 Ponce de Leon Ave
Santurce 00910

Rhode Island

Newport County Community Mental
Health Center, Inc.
174 Bellevue Ave, P.O. Box 116
Newport 02840
(401) 846-1213

Rhode Island Rape Crisis Center, Inc.
235 Promenade St, Rm 202
Providence 02908
(401) 861-4040 (*hotline*);
(401) 723-3050 (*office*)

Women's Liberation Union of Rhode
Island
Committee on Criminal Sex Offenses
P.O. Box 6563, Providence 02940
(401) 861-5511 or 738-2098

South Carolina

People Against Rape
54½ Broad St, Charleston 29401
(803) 722-7273

Rape Education Program
1505 Blanding St, Columbia 29201
(803) 252-2151

Greenville Mental Health Center
715 Grove Rd, Greenville 29605
(803) 242-8085

Rape Crisis Council of Greenville, Inc.
703 E Washington St
Greenville 29601
(803) 232-8633 or 271-0220

Rape Crisis Council of Greenwood
Beckman Center P.O. Drawer 70
Greenwood 29646
(800) 922-4586 (*hotline*);
(803) 223-8331 (*Beckman Center*)

South Greenville Mental Health Center
12 Village Plaza W
Simpsonville 29681
(803) 963-3421

South Dakota

Aberdeen Area Rape Task Force
620 SE 15th Ave, Aberdeen 57401
(605) 225-1010 (*hotline*);
(605) 226-1212 (*office*)

Rape Education, Advocacy and
Counseling Team (REACT)
Brookings Women's Center
802 11th Ave, Brookings 57006
(605) 688-4518 or emergency 911
(*police*)

Victims' Assistance Program
Court Services Department, 7th
Judicial Circuit
703 Adams, Rapid City 57701
(605) 394-2595

Tennessee

Women's Resource and Rape
Assistance Program (WRAP)
238 Summar Dr, Jackson 38301
(901) 668-1764

Knoxville Rape Crisis Center
P.O. Box 9418, Knoxville 37920
(615) 522-7273 (*hotline*);
(615) 522-4745 (*office*)

Comprehensive Rape Crisis Program
1177 Madison, Suite 401
Memphis 38104
(901) 528-2161

Major Crimes
Memphis Police Department
128 Adams, Memphis 38103
(901) 528-2247

Rape and Sexual Abuse Center of
Davidson County
250 Venture Circle, Nashville 37228
Mailing address: P.O. Box 12043
Nashville 37212
(615) 327-1110

Texas

Abilene Rape Crisis Center
P.O. Box 122, Abilene 79604
(915) 677-7895

Mujeres Unidas/Women Together
701 Bowie St, Alamo 78516
(512) 781-3399 (*hotline*);
(512) 383-4959 (*office*)

Rape Crisis and Sexual Abuse Service
804 S Bryan, Suite 218
Amarillo 79106
(806) 373-8022

Austin Child Guidance Center
Services to Exploited Youth Project
510 S Congress, Suite 312
Austin 78704
(512) 472-7273 (*hotline*);
(512) 476-6015 (*office*)

Texas Rape Prevention and Control
Project
P.O. Box 13072, Austin 78711
(512) 476-9887

Rape Crisis Center of Southeast Texas,
Inc.
1310 Broadway #205, P.O. Box 5011
Beaumont 77702
(713) 832-2992

Emergency Room
Medical Center Hospital
301 S 1st St, Conroe 77301
(713) 539-1111

Nueces County Mental Health/Mental
Retardation
Community Center
1630 S Brownlee
Corpus Christi 78404
(512) 888-5321 (*office*);
(512) 888-4445 (*after hours*)

Crimes Against Persons Section
Dallas Police Department
106 S Harwood St, Rm 326
Dallas 75201
(214) 670-5146

Dallas County Rape
Crisis Center
P.O. Box 35728
Dallas 75235
(214) 521-1020

OB-GYN Emergency Room
Parkland Memorial Hospital
5201 Harry Hines Blvd, Dallas 75235
(214) 638-1800 or 2451

Rape Crisis Services
El Paso Mental Health/Mental
Retardation
149 N Raynolds, El Paso 79905
(915) 779-1800 (*hotline*);
(915) 532-6203 (*office*)

Sexual Assault Program
William Beaumont Army
Medical Center
El Paso 79920
(915) 569-2116, 569-2117 or
569-2100

Rape Crisis Support of Tarrant County
P.O. Box 17083, Fort Worth 76102
(817) 336-3355

Emergency Center
Ben Taub General Hospital
1502 Taub Loop, Houston 77030
(713) 791-7300

Harris County District Attorney
Victim/Witness Office
201 Fannin, Rm 200, Houston 77002
(713) 221-6655

Houston Rape Crisis Coalition
Box 4157, Houston 77210
(713) 228-1505

National College of District Attorneys
College of Law
University of Houston
Houston 77004
(713) 488-7222

People Against Rape/Abuse, Inc.
(PARA)
P.O. Box 57535, Houston 77598
(713) 488-7222

Rape Counseling Program
Harris County Health Department
2370 Rice Blvd, Houston 77005
(713) 526-8444

Centex Community Rape Crisis Center
Killeen Community Center
P.O. Box 65, 2001 E Hwy 190
Rm 104
Killeen 76541
(817) 526-6111

Lubbock Rape Crisis Center
P.O. Box 2000, Lubbock 79457
(806) 763-7273 (*hotline*);
(806) 763-3232 (*office*)

Advocacy Program for Victims
of Crime
Department of Human Resources
and Services
City of San Antonio
P.O. Box 9066, San Antonio 78285
(512) 226-4301

Ecumenical Institutional
Services, Inc.
218 S Laredo, San Antonio 78207
(512) 226-6863

Sexual Assault Management Program
Brooke Army Medical Center
Fort Sam Houston,
San Antonio 78234
(512) 221-2225

Smith County Citizens Against Rape,
Inc.
Smith City Rape and Family Crisis
Center
P.O. Box 6302, Tyler 75711
(214) 593-2446

Waco Rape Crisis Center
P.O. Box 464, 201 W Waco Dr
Waco 76703
(817) 752-1113

First Step, Inc.
c/o Joi Garrett
P.O. Box 773, Wichita Falls 76307
Community Relations Office:
600 Scott Street
Wichita Falls 76301
(817) 723-0821 (*hotline*);
(817) 322-1596 (*office*)

Utah

Davis County Family and Community
Mental Health Center
85 S 185 E, Farmington 84025
(801) 867-5581

Rape Crisis Intervention Team
739 N 500 W, Moab 84532
(801) 259-5367

YWCA–Women's Crisis Shelter
505 27th St, Ogden 84403
(801) 392-7273 (*hotline*);
(801) 394-9456 (*office*)

Timpanogos Community Mental
Health Center
1161 E 300 N, Provo 84601
(801) 373-7393

Utah County Rape Crisis Line
P.O. Box 1375, Provo 84601
(801) 375-5111

The Victim Witness Counseling Unit
Salt Lake County Attorney's Office
460 S 3rd E, Salt Lake City 84111
(801) 535-5558

Vermont

Women's Crisis Center
67 Main St, Brattleboro 05301
(802) 254-6954

Women's Rape Crisis Center
P.O. Box 92, Burlington 05401
(802) 863-1236

Rutland County Rape Crisis Team
Box 723, Rutland 05701
(802) 775-1000

Virginia

Fairfax County Victim Assistance
Network
8119 Holland Rd, Alexandria 22306
(703) 360-7273 (*hotline*);
(703) 360-6910 (*office*)

Rape Victim Companion Program
405 Cameron St, P.O. Box 178
Alexandria 22313
(703) 768-1400 (*hotline*);
(703) 750-6631 (*office*)

Arlington County Rape Victim
Companion Service
1725 N George Mason Dr
Arlington 22205
(703) 527-4077 (*hotline*);
(703) 558-2815 (*office*)

Northern Virginia Hotline
P.O. Box 187, Arlington 22210
(703) 527-4077

Charlottesville Rape Crisis Group
214 Rugby Rd, Charlottesville 22901
(804) 977-7273

Rape Crisis Intervention Service
University of Virginia Hospital
203 Davis II, Charlottesville 22903
(804) 924-5564

Tidewater Rape Information Service,
Inc. (TRIS)
230 W Bute St, Norfolk 23510
(804) 622-4300

Crisis Intervention Program
102 N Belvidere St, Richmond 23220
(804) 648-9224

Virginia Committee on Sexual Assault
Reform
3302 W Grace St, Apt 2
Richmond 23221
(804) 353-3392

YWCA Women's Victim Advocacy
Program
6 N 5th St, Richmond 23219
(804) 643-0888 (*hotline*);
(804) 643-6761 (*office*)

TRUST, The Roanoke Valley Trouble
Center
3515 Williamson Rd, Roanoke 24012
(703) 563-0311 (*hotline*);
(703) 345-8859 (*office*)

Western Tidewater Mental Health
Center
428 W Washington St, Suffolk 23434
(804) 539-0238

Washington

Whatcom County Rape Relief
Whatcom County Crisis Services
Mason Bldg, 124 E Holly, Rm 209
Bellingham 98225
(206) 676-1175 (*hotline*);
(206) 671-5754 (*office*)

Rape Response
723 Wallin St, Bremerton 98310
(206) 479-3746

Lewis County Information and
Referral/Hotline
P.O. Box 337, Chehalis 98532
(206) 748-6601

Rape Relief Program of Snohomish
County
Providence Hospital, Pacific and
Nassau
P.O. Box 1067, Everett 98206
(206) 258-7123
(*Providence Hospital*)

Office for Victims of Sexual Assault
Bureau of Community and Residential
Care
Department of Social and Health
Services
OB42A, Olympia 98504
(206) 754-2380;
(235-2380 *Scan*)

Thurston County Rape Relief
YWCA
220 E Union Ave, Olympia 98501
(206) 352–2211 (*hotline*);
(206) 352-0593 (*office*)

Family Support Center
Box 2058, 116 W Apple
Omak 98841
(509) 826-4901

Pullman Rape Resource Line
CUB Student Activities Center
Washington State University
Pullman 99163
(509) 332-4357

King County Rape Relief
305 S 43rd St, Renton 98055
(206) 226-7273 (*hotline*);
(206) 226-0210 or 854-0523 (*office*)

Mid-Columbia Rape Relief and Sexual
Assault Program
1175 Gribble St, Richland 99352
(509) 943-9104

Crisis Clinic, Inc.
United Way Information and Referral
1530 Eastlake Ave E, Seattle 98102
(206) 325-5550 (hotline);
(206) 323-2100 (referrals);
(206) 329-1882 (office)

Division of Family, Women and
Children's Services
Department of Human Resources
400 Yesler, Seattle 98104
(206) 625-4516

Feminist Karate Union
Rape Prevention and Self Protection
Workshop
101 Nickerson, Suite 250A
Seattle 98109
(206) 282-0177

Prevention of Sexual Violence Project
4250 S Mead St, Seattle 98118
(206) 723-4750

Seattle Police Academy (Training
Center)
1201 S 104th, Seattle 98122
(206) 625-4684

Seattle Rape Relief
4224 University Way, NE
Seattle 98105
(206) 632-7273

Sexual Assault Center
325 Ninth Ave, Seattle 98104
(206) 223-3047 (days);
(206) 223-3010 (nights, weekends;
ask for social worker)

Program for Sexual Adjustment
Spokane Community Mental
Health Center
S 107 Division, Spokane 99202
(509) 838-4651

Rape Crisis Network
N 1226 Howard St, Spokane 99201
(509) 624-7273

Pierce County Rape Relief
Allenmore Medical Center
Suite A105
S 19th & Union, Tacoma 98405
(206) 627-1135

Community Assault and Abuse Center
216 S Palouse St (drop-in center)
420 W Poplar, Walla Walla 99362
(509) 529-3377 (hotline);
(509) 525-0241 (drop-in center)

Wenatchee Rape Crisis Center
Chelan County Special Services Center
327 Okanogan St, Wenatchee 98801
(509) 663-7446

Central Washington Comprehensive
Mental Health Center
Rape Relief Program
321 E Yakima Ave, P.O. Box 959,
Yakima 98907
(509) 575-4200

West Virginia

Sexual Assault Information
Center, Inc.
1036 Quarrier St, #317
Charleston 25301
(304) 344-9834 (hotline);
(304) 344-9839 (office)

Community Mental Health Center
Region II
3375 Rt 60 E, Huntington 25705
(304) 525-7851

Rape and Domestic Violence
Information Center
P.O. Box 4228, Morgantown 26505
(304) 599-6800

Rape Information and Counseling
Service
P.O. Box 2033, Parkersburg 26101
(304) 485-9700

Hancock-Brooke Mental Health Service
P.O. Box 2010, Weirton 26062
(304) 723-5440

Wisconsin

Sexual Assault Crisis Center—Fox
Cities
P.O. Box 344, Appleton 54912
(414) 733-8119

Northern Community Mental Health
Center
1923 Beaser Ave, Ashland 54806
(715) 682-8114

Green Bay Rape Crisis Center, Ltd.
744 S Webster, P.O. Box 1700,
Green Bay 54305
(414) 468-3553

Jefferson County Human Services
P.O. Box 375, Jefferson 53545
(414) 674-3105

New Horizons–YWCA Women's
Center
P.O. Box 2031, LaCrosse 54601
(608) 784-6419

Dane County Project on Rape
120 W Mifflin St, Madison 53703
(608) 251-5440

Rape Crisis Center, Inc.
P.O. Box 1312, Madison 53701
(608) 251-7273

University of Wisconsin Department of
Police and Security
101 N Mills St, Madison 53706
(608) 262-4889

Wisconsin Division of Corrections
Bureau of Program Resources
P.O. Box 669, Madison 53701
(608) 266-2789

Women's Transit Authority
306 N Brooks St, Madison 53715
(608) 256-3710 (*days*);
(608) 263-1700 (*nights, rides*)

Marinette General Hospital
3100 Shore Dr, Marinette 54143
(715) 735-6621

Family Planning Information and
Referral Service, Planned Parenthood
1135 W State St, Milwaukee 53233
(800) 242-9922 (*toll-free*);
(414) 271-8181 (*office*)

Witness Support/Sexual Assault
Counseling Unit
District Attorney's Office
821 W State St, Milwaukee 53233
(414) 278-4617

Women's Crisis Line
1428 N Farwell Ave
Milwaukee 53202
(414) 964-7535 (*hotline*);
(414) 271-8112 (*office*)

Winnebago County Rape Crisis Center
404 N Main St, Oshkosh 54901
(414) 426-1460

Women's Resource Center
740 College Ave, Racine 53403
(414) 633-3233

Emergency Room
St. Michael's Hospital
900 Illinois Ave, Stevens Point 54481
(715) 344-4400

Women's Resource Center, Inc.
2101A Main St, Stevens Point 54481
(715) 346-4851

Kenoshans Against Sexual Assault, Inc.
(KASA)
c/o Linda Marcussen
Rt 1, Box 103X, Trevor 53179
(414) 658-1717

Domestic Abuse and Sexual Assault
Victim Services, Inc. (D.A.S.A.V.S.)
P.O. Box 172, Wausau 54401
(715) 842-7323 (*hotline*);
(715) 842-7636 (*office*)

Wyoming

Western Wyoming Mental Health
Association
115 W Snowking Ave, P.O. Box 1868
Jackson 83001
(307) 733-2046;
(800) 442-6383 (*toll-free*)

Sweetwater County Task Force on
Sexual Assault
450 S Main, Rocksprings 82901
(307) 382-4381

Confidential Assistance Line
Box 1321, Worland 82401
(307) 347-2674

CANADA

Alberta

Rape Crisis Centre of Edmonton
416-10010-105 St
Edmonton T5J 1C4
(403) 429-0023

British Columbia

Naniamo Rape Relief Centre
361 Vancouver Ave
Naniamo V9S 4G3
(604) 753-0022 (*hotline*);
(604) 753-1021 (*office*)

Vancouver Anti-Sexual Assault Centre
4–45 Kingsway, Vancouver V5T 3H7
(604) 732-1613 (*hotline*)

Manitoba

Rape Crisis and Information,Centre
(Klinic, Inc.)
545 Broadway Ave
Winnipeg R3C OW3
(204) 774-4525 (*hotline*);
(204) 786-6943 (*office*)

New Brunswick

Fredericton Rape Crisis Service
P.O. Box 1033, Fredericton
New Brunswick E3B 5C2
(506) 454-0437

Newfoundland

St. John's Rape Crisis and Information
Centre
P.O. Box 6072, St. John's A1C 5X8
(709) 726-1411 (*hotline*);
(709) 753-0220 (*office*)

Ontario

Women in Crisis
University of Guelph
P.O. Box 43, U.G.C.S.A.
Guelph N1G 2V7
(519) 836-5710

Women in Crisis
177 Norfolk St, P.O. Box 1451
Guelph
(519) 836-5710 (*hotline*);
(519) 836-1110 (*office*)

CARSA
Niagara Region Sexual Assault Centre
5017 Victoria Ave
Niagara Falls L2E 4C9
(416) 356-9662

Ottawa Rape Crisis Centre
P.O. Box 35, Station B, Ottawa
(613) 238-6666 (*hotline*);
(613) 238-6667 (*office*)

Thunder Bay Rape and Sexual Assault
Centre
316 Bay St, P.O. Box 314 TBF
Thunder Bay
(807) 344-4502

Toronto Rape Crisis Centre
Box 6597, Postal Station A
Toronto M5W 1X4
(416) 964-8080 (*hotline*);
(416) 964-7477 (*office*)

Sexual Assault Crisis Clinic
Windsor Western Hospital
Out-Patient Clinics
Windsor N9C 3Z4
(519) 253-9667 (*hotline*);
(519) 253-4261, ext 298 (*office*)

Quebec

Montreal Women's Aid
C.P. 82, Station E, Montreal
(514) 270-8291

Saskatchewan

Regina Women's Community Centre
and Rape Crisis Line
1810 Smith St, Rm 219
Regina S4P 1X7
(306) 352-0434